ST. MARKS PLAZA, VENICE: *Colonnade of the Procuratie Nuove (from the painting by Canaletto in the National Gallery, London)*

Photographed from an illustration in "Painting in Oils" by Bertram Nicholls, The Studio Publications, Inc., London and New York (1938)

THE ART OF BUILDING CITIES

city building
according to its
artistic fundamentals

By CAMILLO SITTE

TRANSLATED BY

CHARLES T. STEWART

Martino Publishing
Mansfield Centre, CT
2013

Martino Publishing
P.O. Box 373,
Mansfield Centre, CT 06250 USA

ISBN   978-1-61427-524-4

© *2013 Martino Publishing*

Cover design by T. Matarazzo

Printed in the United States of America On 100% Acid-Free Paper

THE ART OF BUILDING CITIES

city building
according to its
artistic fundamentals

By CAMILLO Sitte

TRANSLATED BY

CHARLES T. STEWART

REINHOLD PUBLISHING CORPORATION

330 WEST 42ND STREET

NEW YORK, N. Y.

1945

Printed in U. S. A. by Ar-Kay Printing Co., Inc.

A NOTE ON CAMILLO SITTE

In the closing years of the last century, Sitte's book on town building was widely familiar among architects of that generation, particularly in the German speaking countries and in Northern Europe. As a result, a strong groundwork was laid for an architectural understanding of the fact that the building must be an integral part of an environment of such organic town pattern as is expressive of contemporary conditions, and of no other conditions. Simultaneously with this understanding of organic town pattern, and subsequently to a great extent as a logical consequence of it—although Sitte himself did not particularly stress this point, or perhaps was not even in those days of imitation distinctly aware of it—there became laid an equally strong groundwork for such an understanding of architecture that even the architectural style-form must express contemporary conditions, and no other conditions. This brought the prevailing architectural education of that super-stylistic "Beaux-Arts" order into disrepute, and a search for a new form-expression became widespread and alive.

Just in these years (1896) I started my architectural practice. And, as I had become animated from the very start by the core of Sitte's teachings, it then so happened that during my subsequent architectural practice of almost half a century I never have designed and executed any buildings in a preconceived style-form. I simply could not do it. More than that: during all this long period of time, it has been simply impossible for me to regard a building of borrowed and alien style-form—no matter how magnificent—as belonging to the realm of the art of building, but only as a product of "building trade," enveloped in a jacket of meaningless decoration. This has been by no means conceit on my part. Rather, it has been just as truly an indigenous and intense feeling within me as is that feeling truly indigenous and intense within any child that a strange, cold, and unconcerned damsel, trimmed in pretentious attire, is not one's mother. I have been satisfied with this feeling. And I am sure that I have this feeling, to a great extent, thanks to Sitte's teaching, through which I learned to undertsand those laws of architecture that are from time immemorial.

Surely, this is the highest tribute that I personally can pay to Sitte's book on town building.

In the chapter, "Informal Revival," of my book *THE CITY* I have endeavored a short analysis of Sitte's ideas. I am now pleased to know that Sitte's book *in extenso* will be available in English translation.

Indeed, it is not too early!

ELIEL SAARINEN

Cranbrook Academy of Art
February, 1944

Translator's Preface

A literal, if cumbersome, translation of the title of this book would be "City Building According To Its Artistic Fundamentals." It was written by Camillo Sitte, a Viennese architect, and first appeared in 1889 to burst like a demolition bomb on the city planning practices of Europe. Its attack upon monotony and dreariness in city arrangement precipitated a revolt against unimaginative formality which Mr. Eliel Saarinen regards as the "informal revival" in city planning—the effort to restore fundamental but forgotten principles in civic design.

Sitte's work has been translated into French and Spanish. Although it has not previously appeared in English, it has exercised a persistent, although necessarily a diminished, influence in English speaking countries. It is presented, even half a century late, to American readers because it has much that is timely to say to us in a day that is marked for the structural rebirth of our cities. Sitte's mighty scorn for the uninspiring practices of his day retains its cauterizing sting for ours. While some of his specific suggestions may need reappraisal in the light of new elements in urban living that have been introduced since he lived and wrote, the essentials of his book, the "artistic fundamentals," have not been invalidated by the passage of time.

Rebuilding of cities has become a vital subject in America. It has a prominent and urgent place on our post-war agenda. Preparations being made for it are largely legalistic and financial. When the decks have been cleared of these fiscal preliminaries, we shall be face to face with the practical problem of rebuilding our cities in good taste as well as for efficiency and economy. We shall then find *The Art of Building Cities* as timely as the morning paper.

My thanks are due to Mr. Herbert U. Nelson for encouragement to prepare the translation; to Mr. Eliel Saarinen, Mr. Ralph Walker, and Mr. Arthur Holden for their valued contributions to the volume; to Mr. Kenneth Reid and Mr. Gessner G. Hawley for numerous editorial suggestions; to the Harvard University Library and Avery Library of Columbia University for the protracted loan of the fourth edition of Sitte's *Der Städtebau* and the French version of Camille Martin.

CHARLES T. STEWART

Washington, D. C.
September 17, 1944

v

Introduction to the English Translation

by Ralph Walker

THE present day qualities of the city were well envisioned in 1889 by Sitte. The monotonous building lines, the endless streets, the rigid gridiron, the small amount of open space, were all indicated to him in the trends toward the engineer-controlled city. The lack of coordinated design, even in the few sterile attempts at the grandiose which were attempted, proved a poverty of imagination which could but lead to the now all too evident ugly city.

The growing number of comforts within the modern shelter had, one by one, eliminated the desire for pageantry in the space outside. The underlying idea of the forum and the plaza, throughout the ages the focal points of classical and medieval cities, took on less social and political meaning. This was followed, unfortunately, by an introversion of citizen interest so that here, too, there was lost an active sense of participation in those urban affairs which directly affected his welfare.

The rulers of great cities which sprawled over and obliterated active and normal village life, forgot that unless a city developed the art of living within itself, forgot that unless it further developed the physical and emotional qualities in a visual art vital to its citizens, the citizens might seek, as they have, other places where these qualities could be found.

Sitte offers an esthetic approach intended to bring about, within the city, an outdoor life possessing intellectual and emotional stimuli. His analysis of the faults underlying the trends toward gigantic and chaotic urban growth are as profound today as they were at the end of the last century. He condemned the long and purposeless vista, the lack of emotional interest in the rigid building lines inherent in speculative land promotion, foreseeing that this would lead to a "cube motif" in architecture and finally to a city where people would be hived and warehoused rather than one where an active citizen participation might be encouraged through a pride and satisfaction in the place of living.

The modern engineer city philosophy, at present so influential, develops naturally into the great walls of Corbusier's "City of Tomorrow," of "La Ville Radieuse," and which can best be described as: From cell to cell—a cell in a housing hill to a cell in a larger heap (the mass production factory or the skyscraper); from artificial life to artificial work, dwellers and workers in cells, travelers in cells. Utopia is the promise that all these monotonous cells belong to the dictatorship of the "little men" who occupy them. Here, indeed, is logic untempered by humanity.

Every community needs a symbol of its existence. Much of modern community frustration has come into being because a symbol of the visual reason for its life is missing. Because no symbol is found there is no center on which to focus life.

The social and esthetic problem facing every large city in America and needing solution is how to take the deadly gridiron plan and remold it into a greater freedom and a larger quality of community integration. The present concept of a quiet island community surrounded by and at the same time insulated from arterial highways, and served within by a broken pattern of roads and open spaces designed to limit speed, needs a designer fully conscious of the need for social and esthetic composition as well as for the utilities which make for comfort and sanitary safety.

The fact that so many of the examples which Sitte uses from the cities of the past are relatively small in scale has for our time many sound psychological meanings, because where the citizen hitherto has been active in the development of urban cultures the scale of his community has been related and comprehensible to him. He, therefore, has been able to receive in return as great a stimulus as he imparts.

It is then in this return to human comprehension and scale that Sitte suggests there will be found not only the needed sanity and repose in contrast to the neurosis inherent in the megalomanian scale of the unplanned modern city, but also those community qualities with which we may develop a more satisfactory urban design in the future.

Sitte's ideas concerning community scale and esthetic order bring into sharp relief some of the fallacies in the design philosophy so prevalent in the many zoning ordinances throughout the country, one of which, for example, is the insistence upon a uniform front yard. The monotony so characteristic of the modern city is thus embedded in law. In the "quiet island" the streets need be designed for minor local and slow traffic only, thereby permitting community arrangements which focus attention on composed relationships and pleasant vistas rather than on the endless sky ahead. To effect this will require a greater freedom under the zoning laws, and a larger responsibility granted planning groups. We now see a growing appreciation of this need for design develop in large projects, but the great amount of building under existing laws is still sited on antiquated principles of urban esthetics, as well as on dangerous principles of street design.

Sitte's book, moreover, points up the contrast between the actual design of the classical city with its conscious appreciation of composed impressions and the so-called monumental and symmetrical effects inherent in the use of the drafting board center axis; the contrast between those who worked with and on the site itself and those others who must always change the flow of nature into symmetrical sterility.

It should not be forgotten that the scale of open spaces is definitely related to the mass and quality of the buildings which surround them. Formality or informality of space design are not to be achieved by arbitrary decisions, they have natural associations. The free country-like landscaped park which fits the low skyline of London would seem out of place in cities where buildings are taller and which therefore, because of greater architectural masses, demand a more formal treatment. Nor need this quality become unnecessarily grandiose.

The modern city form under the pressure caused by the deserts of masonry has become increasingly chaotic in its widespread decentralization. At the same time there has been everywhere an increasing demand for a return to outdoor life; because the greater leisure possible under modern production methods has created a need for recreational areas. The city which, in the past, seemed because of its complete congestion impossible of achieving any of the needed open spaces except at great cost, will find at present many opportunities in the operation of building and neighborhood obsolescence. Fortunately the opportunity and the knowledge of the extent of the required need are in parallel.

How the opportunity is accepted, how enduring the results, will depend largely upon the philosophy under which the projects are designed. Sitte offers one way of achievement which is as usable today as it was in the past in insuring a consistent stability. The American architect and planner will owe a great deal to Charles Stewart for the first and very excellent and complete translation into English of Sitte's book. They will find it of greater value the more the present monotony persists.

CONTENTS

MEMORY of travel is the stuff of our fairest dreams. Splendid cities, plazas, monuments, and landscapes thus pass before our eyes, and we enjoy again the charming and impressive spectacles that we have formerly experienced. If we could but stop again at those places where beauty never satiates, we could bear many dreary hours with a light heart and pursue life's long struggle with new energies. Assuredly the imperturbable lightheartedness of the South, on the Hellenic coast, in lower Italy and other favored climes, is above all a gift of nature. And the old cities of these countries, built after the beauty of nature itself, continue to augment nature's gentle and irresistible influence upon the soul of man. Only the person who has never understood the beauty of an ancient city could contradict this assertion.

Let him go ramble on the ruins of Pompeii to convince himself of it. If, after a day of patient investigation there, he walks across the bare Forum, he will be drawn, in spite of himself, to the summit of the monumental staircase toward the terrace of Jupiter's temple. On this platform, which dominates the entire place, he will sense, rising within him, waves of harmony like the pure, full tones of sublime music. Under this influence he will truly understand the words of Aristotle, who thus summarized all principles of city building: "A city should be built to give its inhabitants security and happiness."

The science of the technician will not suffice to accomplish this. We need, in addition, the talent of the artist. Thus it was in ancient times, in the Middle Ages, and in the Renaissance, wherever fine arts were held in esteem. It is only in our mathematical century that the construction and extension of cities has become a purely technical matter. Perhaps, then, it is not beside the point to recall that these problems have diverse aspects, and that he who has been given the least attention in our time is perhaps not the least important.

The object of this study, then, is clear. It is not our purpose to republish ancient and trite ideas, nor to reopen sterile complaints against the already proverbial banality of modern streets. It is useless to hurl general condemnations and to put everything that has been done in our time and place once more to the pillory. That kind of purely negative effort should be left to the critic who is never satisfied and who

1

can only contradict. Those who have enough enthusiasm and faith in good causes should be convinced that our own era can create works of beauty and worth. We shall examine the plans of a number of cities, but neither as historian nor as critic. We wish to seek out, as technician and artist, the elements of composition which formerly produced such harmonious effects, and those which today produce only loose and dull results. Perhaps this study will permit us to find the means of satisfying the three principal requirements of practical city building: to rid the modern system of blocks and regularly aligned houses; to save as much as possible of that which remains from ancient cities; and in our creation to approach more closely the ideal of the ancient models.

This standpoint of practical art will lead us to consider especially the cities of the Middle Ages and the Renaissance. We shall be content, on recalling examples from Greek and Roman conceptions, either to explain the creations of following epochs, or to support the ideas that we propose to develop. For the principal architectural elements of cities have greatly changed since antiquity. Public squares (Forum, market, etc.) are used in our times not so much for great popular festivals or for the daily needs of our life. The sole reason for their existence is to provide more air and light, and to break the monotony of oceans of houses. At times they also enhance a monumental edifice by freeing its walls. It was quite different in ancient times. Public squares, or plazas, were then of prime necessity, for they were theaters for the principal scenes of public life, which today take place in enclosed halls. Under the open sky, on the agora, the council of the ancient Greeks gathered.

The market place, a further center of activity for our ancestors, has persisted, it is true, to the present time, but more and more it is being replaced by vast enclosed halls. And how many other scenes of public life have totally disappeared? Sacrifices before the temples, games, and theatrical presentations of all kinds. The temples themselves were scarcely covered, and the principal part of dwellings, around which were grouped large and small rooms, consisted of an open court. In a word, the distinction between the public square and other structures was so slight that it is amazing to our modern minds, accustomed to a very different state of things.

A review of the writings of the period proves to us that the ancients themselves sensed this similarity. Thus Vitruvius does not discuss the Forum in connection with the placement of public buildings or the arrangement of streets in his account of Dinocrates and his plan of Alexandria. But he does mention it in the same chapter which discusses the Basilica, and in the same book (I, 5.) he deals with the theaters, palaces, the circus, and the baths. That is to say, all gathering places under the open sky constituted architectural works. The ancient Forum corresponds exactly to this definition, and Vitruvius logically places it in this group. This close relationship between the Forum and a public hall enhanced architecturally by statues and paintings is brought out clearly by the Latin writer's description, and more clearly still by an examination of the Forum of Pompeii. Vitruvius writes again on this subject:

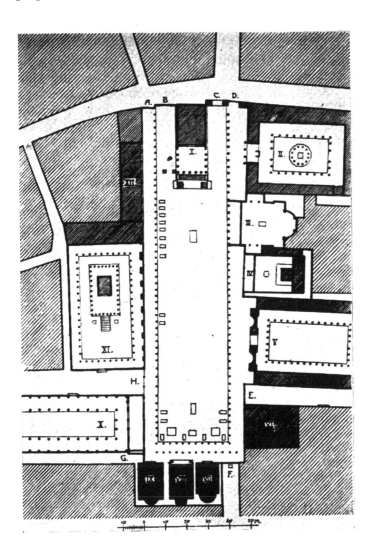

1

FORUM OF POMPEII

I Temple of Jupiter, II Enclosed Market, III Temple of Household Gods, IV Temple of Vespasianus, V Eumachia, VI Comitium, VII-IX Public Buildings, X Basilica, XI Temple of Apollo, XII Market Hall.

"The Greeks arrange their market places in the form of a square and surround them by vast double columns supporting stone or marble architraves above which run the promenades. In Italian cities the Forum takes another aspect, for from time immemorial it has been the theater of gladiatorial combats. The columns, therefore, must be less densely grouped. They shelter the stalls of the silversmiths, and their upper floors have projections in the form of balconies which are advantageously placed for frequent use and for public revenue."

This description illustrates well the correspondence between theater and Forum. This relationship appears still more striking when we examine the plan of the Forum of Pompeii *(Figure 1)*. The square is surrounded on all sides by public buildings. The temple of Jupiter alone rises in isolation. And the two-story colonnade which surrounds the entire space is interrupted only by the peristyle of the temple of the household gods, which makes a greater projection than the other buildings. The center of the Forum remains free, but its periphery is occupied by numerous monuments, the pedestals of which, covered with inscriptions, are still visible.

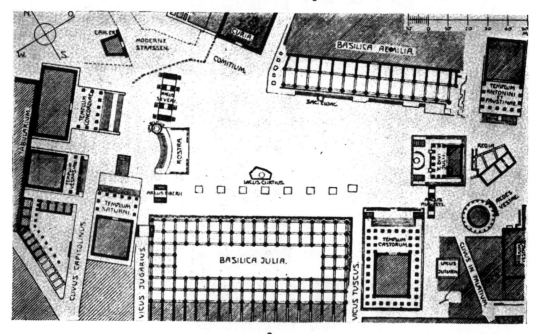

2
FORUM ROMANUM

Author's Introduction

What a grandiose impression this place must have made! To our modern point of view its effect is like that of a great concert hall without ceiling. In every direction the eye fell upon edifices which in no respect resembled our files of modern houses, and there were far fewer streets opening directly on the plaza. Streets ran behind buildings III, IV, and V, but they did not extend as far as the Forum. Streets C, D, E, and F were closed by grilles, and even those on the north side passed under the monumental portals, A and B.

Forum Romanum *(Figure 2)* was conceived according to the same principles. It is surrounded, of course, by buildings more varied in type but all monumental. The streets which open onto it were arranged to avoid too frequent openings in the frame of the plaza. Monuments are located around its sides rather than in its center. In brief, the place of the forum in cities corresponds to that of the principal room of a house. It is to the city, so to speak, the principal hall, as well arranged as it is richly furnished. There stand assembled in immense bulk the

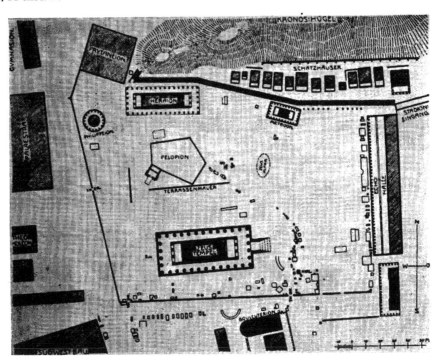

3

THE TEMPLE OF ZEUS AND PLAZA OF OLYMPIA

columns, the statues, the monuments, and everything that can contribute to the splendor of the place. The art treasures of some of them were said to be numbered in hundreds and thousands. As they did not encumber the midst of the plaza, but were always located at the periphery, it was possible to encompass them all with a single glance, and the spectacle must have been imposing. This concentration of plastic and architectural masterpieces at a single point was a stroke of genius. Aristotle had taught it. He advocated grouping the temples of the gods with public buildings. Pausanias wrote similarly, "A city without public edifices and squares is not worthy of its name."

The market place of Athens is arranged in its principal features according to the same rules, as well as may be judged from the restoration projects. They are applied on a still grander scale in the consecrated cities of Hellenic antiquity (Olympia, Delphi, Eleusis) *(Figure 3)*. Masterpieces of architecture, painting, and sculpture are found there in a superb and imposing union capable of rivaling the most powerful tragedies and the most majestic symphonies. The Acropolis of Athens *(Figure 4)* is the most finished creation of this character. A high plateau surrounded by high walls is the base of it. The lower entrance portal, the enormous flight of steps, and monumen-

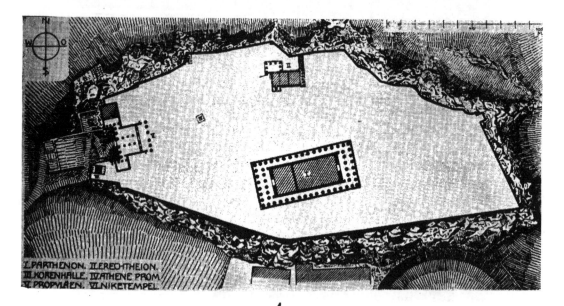

4

THE ACROPOLIS OF ATHENS IN THE AGE OF PERICLES

tal vestibules constitute the first phrase of this symphony in marble, gold, ivory, bronze, and color. The interior temples and monuments are the stone myths of the Greek people. The highest poetry and thought are embodied in them. It is truly the center of a considerable city, an expression of the feelings of a great people. It is no longer a simple square in the ordinary sense of the term, but the work of several centuries grown to the maturity of pure art.

It is impossible to establish a higher aim in this style, and it is difficult to imitate successfully this splendid model, but it should always remain before our eyes in all our works as the most sublime ideal to attain. In the progress of our study we shall see that the principles which have inspired such building are not entirely lost, but that they remain to us.

I

The Relationship Between Buildings, Monuments, and Public Squares

IN the South of Europe, and especially in Italy, where ancient cities and ancient public customs have remained alive for ages, even to the present in some places, public squares still follow the type of the ancient forum. They have preserved their role in public life. Their natural relationships with the buildings which enclose them may still be readily discerned. The distinction between the forum, or agora, and the market place also remains. As before, we find the tendency to concentrate outstanding buildings at a single place, and to ornament this center of community life with fountains, monuments, and statues which can bring back historical memories and which, during the Middle Ages and the Renaissance, constituted the glory and pride of each city.

It was there that traffic was most intense. That is where public festivals and theatrical presentations were held. There it was that official ceremonies were conducted and laws promulgated. In Italy, according to varying circumstances, two or three public places, rarely a single one, served these practical purposes.

The existence of two powers, temporal and spiritual, required two distinct centers: one, the cathedral square (*Figure 5*) dominated by the campanile, the baptistry, and the palace of the bishop; the other, the Signoria, or manor place, which is a kind of vestibule to a royal residence. It is enclosed by houses of the country's great

5

PISA: Cathedral Square

a. Saint-Jean   b. Cathedral
c. Campanile   d. Campo Santo (Cemetery)

and adorned with monuments. Sometimes we see there a loggia, or open gallery, used by a military guard, or a high terrace from which laws and public statements were promulgated. The Signoria of Florence (*Figure 6*) is the finest example of this. The market square, rarely lacking even in cities of northern Europe, is the meeting place of the citizens. There stand the City Hall and the more or less richly decorated traditional fountain, the sole vestige of the past that has been conserved since the lively activity of merchants and traders has been moved within to iron cages and glass market places.

this. It includes everything that the people of the City have been able to create in building religious edifices of unparalleled richness and grandeur. The splendid cathedral, the campanile, the baptistry, the incomparable Campo-Santo are not depreciated by profane or banal surroundings of any kind. The effect produced by such a

6

FLORENCE, Piazza of the Signoria

The important function of the public square in the community life of past ages is evident. The period of the Renaissance saw the birth of masterpieces in the manner of the Acropolis of Athens, where everything concurred to produce a finished artistic effect. The cathedral place at Pisa, an Acropolis of Pisa, *(Figure 5)* is the proof of

place, removed from the world of baseness while rich in the noblest works of the human spirit, is overpowering. Even those with a poorly developed sensitiveness to art are unable to escape the power of this impression. There is nothing there to distract our thoughts or to intrude our daily affairs. The esthetic enjoyment of those who look upon

9

the noble façade of the Cathedral is not spoiled by the sight of a modern haberdashery, by the cries of drivers and porters, or by the tumult of a café. Peace reigns over the place. It is thus possible to give full attention to the art work assembled there.

This situation is almost unique, although that of Saint Francis of Assissi and the arrangement of the Certosa de Pavia closely approach it. In general, the modern period does not encourage the formation of such perfect groupings. Cities, even in the fatherland of art, undergo the fate of palaces and dwellings. They no longer have distinct character. They present a mixture of motifs borrowed as much from the architecture of the north as from that of the southern countries. Ideas and tastes have been mingled as the people themselves have been interchanged. Local characteristics are gradually disappearing. The market place alone, with its City Hall and fountain, has here and there remained intact.

In passing we should like to remark that our intention is not to suggest a sterile imitation of the beauties spoken of as "picturesque" in the ancient cities for our present needs. The proverb, "Necessity breaks even iron," is fully applicable here. Changes made necessary by hygiene or other requirements must be carried out, even if the picturesque suffers from it. But that does not prevent us from examining the work of our forebears at close range to determine how much of it may be adapted to modern conditions. In this way alone can we resolve the esthetic part of the practical problem of city building, and determine what can be saved from the heritage of our ancestors.

Before determining the question in a positive manner, we state the principle that during the Middle Ages and Renaissance public squares were often used for practical purposes, and that they formed an entirely with the buildings which enclosed them. Today they serve at best as places for stationing vehicles, and they have no relation to the buildings which dominate them. Our parliament buildings have no agora enclosed by columns. Our universities and cathedrals have lost their atmosphere of peace. Surging throngs no longer circulate on market days before our City Halls. In brief, activity is lacking precisely in those places where, in ancient times, it was most intense—near public structures. Thus, to a great extent, we have lost that which contributed to the splendor of public squares.

And the fabric of their very splendor, the numerous statues, is almost entirely lacking today. What have we to compare to the richness of ancient forums and to works of majestic style like the Signoria of Florence and its Loggia dei Lanzi?

A few years ago there flourished at Vienna a remarkable school of sculpture whose works of merit cannot be scorned. They were generally used to adorn buildings. In only a few exceptional cases were their works used in public squares. Statues adorn the two museums, the palace of Parliament, the two Court theaters, the City

Hall, the new university, the Votive Church. But there is no interest in adorning public open spaces. And that is true not only in Vienna, but nearly everywhere.

Buildings lay claim to so many statues that commissions are needed to find new subjects to be represented. It is often necessary to wait for years to find a suitable place for a statue although many appropriate places remain empty in the meantime. After long efforts we have reconciled ourselves to modern public squares as vast as they are deserted, and the monument, without a place of refuge, becomes stranded on some small and ancient space. That is even more strange, yet true. After much groping about, this fortunate result occurs, for it is thus that a work of art derives its value and produces a more powerful impression. Indifferent artists who neglect to provide for such effects must bear the entire responsibility of it.

The story of Michelangelo's *David* at Florence shows how mistakes of this kind are perpetrated in modern times. This gigantic marble statue stands close to the walls of the Palazzo Vecchio, to the left of its principal entrance, in the exact place chosen by Michelangelo. The idea of erecting a statue on this place of ordinary appearance would have appeared to moderns as absurd if not insane. Michelangelo chose it, however, and without doubt deliberately; for all those who have seen the masterpiece in this place testify to the extraordinary impression that it makes. In contrast to the relative scantiness of the place, affording an easy comparison with human stature, the enormous statue seems to swell even beyond its actual dimensions. The sombre and uniform, but powerful, walls of the palace provide a background on which we could not wish to improve to make all the lines of the figure stand out.

Today the *David* is moved into one of the academy's halls under a glass cupola in the midst of plaster reproductions, photographs, and engravings. It serves as a model for study and an object of research for historians and critics. A special mental preparation is needed now to resist the morbid influences of an art prison that we call a museum, and to have the ability to enjoy the imposing work. Moreover, the spirit of the times, which believed that it was perfecting art, and which was still not satisfied with this innovation, had a bronze cast made of the *David* in its original grandeur and put it up on a vast plaza (naturally in its mathematical center) far from Florence at the Via dei Colli. It has a superb horizon before it; behind it, cafes; on one side, a carriage station, a corso; and from all sides the murmurs of Baedeker readers ascend to it. In this setting the statue produces no effect at all. The opinion that its dimensions do not exceed human stature is often heard. Michelangelo thus understood best the kind of placement that would be suitable for his work, and, in general, the ancients were abler than we are in these matters.

The fundamental difference between

11

the procedures of former times and those of today rests in the fact that we constantly seek the largest possible space for each little statue. Thus we diminish the effect that it could produce, instead of augmenting it with the assistance of a neutral background such as painters have used in their portraits.

This explains why the ancients erected their monuments by the sides of public places, as is shown in the view of the Signoria of Florence. In this way, the number of statues could increase indefinitely without obstructing the circulation of traffic, and each of them had a fortunate background. Contrary to this, we hold the middle of a public place as the sole spot worthy to receive a monument. Thus no esplanade, however magnificent, can have more than one. If by misfortune it is irregular and if its center cannot be located geometrically we become confused and allow the space to remain empty for eternity.

II

IT is instructive to study the manner in which the ancients located their fountains and monuments and to see how they were always able to make use of the conditions at hand. Ancient principles of art were applied anew in the Middle Ages, although less obviously. Only blindness can escape the observation that the Romans left the center of their forum free. Even in Vitruvius we may read that the center of a public place is destined not for statues but for gladiators. This question calls for a more attentive study of the following epochs.

In the Middle Ages the choice of placing fountains and statues together in many cases defies all definition. Some of the strangest arrangements were adopted. It is always necessary to recognize that, as for Michelangelo's *David*, this choice was guided by a fine sense for art, for the statue always harmonized admirably with its surroundings. Thus we face an enigma, the enigma of a natural art sense which, among the old masters, wrought miracles without the assistance of any esthetic rules. Modern technicians, who have succeeded them, armed with T-squares and compasses, have pretended to make fine decisions of taste through the coarseness of geometry.

Sometimes it is possible to catch a glimpse of the creative methods of our forebears and to find words that can explain the patterns of the successful effects that they attained. But since particular examples can vary so widely it seems difficult to wrest a general principle from the known facts. We shall try to see clearly in this apparent confusion, however, for our innate feeling has been lost for a long time. We can no longer get good results without deliberate intention. If, then, we wish to rediscover the free inventiveness of the old masters and react against the inflexible geometrical principles of their successors, we must make an effort to follow the paths over which our ancestors went by instinct in ages that had a traditional esteem for art.

The subject of this chapter seems narrowly limited. Nevertheless, it is difficult to cover it in a few words. An example taken from everyday life which we hope is not shocking in its apparent triviality will make a useful substitute for an involved definition.

It is remarkable how children, working with no direction except their artistic instinct, often achieve the same results as primitive peoples in their crude designs. It may be surprising to say that one of their favorite games can teach us the principles of good monument location. As a matter of

13

fact, the snowmen with which they amuse themselves in the winter are located in exactly the same manner as fountains and monuments were according to ancient practices. The explanation is quite simple. Consider the snow covered plaza of a town.

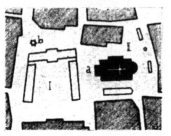

7

NUREMBERG

I Market Square
II Frauen Plaza
a. Marienkirche
b. Fountain

Here and there are snow paths—natural thoroughfares. There are large blocks of snow irregularly located between them, and the snowmen are built on these, for that is where the substance of which they are made is found.

It was at such points, similarly dispersed from traffic, that the ancient communities set up their fountains and monuments. It may be observed from old engravings that in ancient times the public places were not paved, nor even graded, but were furrowed in paths and gutters, as may still be seen in certain villages. If the building of a fountain were desired, it obviously would not be located on a thoroughfare, but rather on one of the island-like plots separated from traffic. When, with an increase in wealth, the community grew little by little, it had its public places graded and paved, but the fountain did not change its position.

When it was desired to replace it by a similar, but more elaborate, structure, the new one was put up on the same spot.

Thus, each of these sites had its historical importance, and this explains why fountains and monuments are not located at places of intense traffic use, nor at the center of public places, nor on the axis of a monumental portal, but by preference to the side, even in the northern countries where Latin traditions have not had a direct influence. This also explains why in each city and in each public place the arrangement of monuments is different, for in each case streets open onto the square differently; traffic follows a different direction and leaves other points free. In short, the historical development of the public square varies according to the locality. It sometimes happens that the center of a public

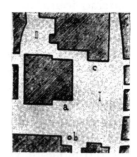

8

ROTHENBURG ON TAUBER

I. Market Square
b. City Hall
b. Fountain
c. Cafe

place is selected for the placement of a statue, but this practice, preferred by modern architects, was never established as a principle by the ancients.

They were not given to the excessive use of symmetry, for their fountains were built most frequently near the angle of a public square, where the principal street opened and where draft animals were brought for watering. The beautiful fountain of Nuremberg *(Figure 7)* is a celebrated

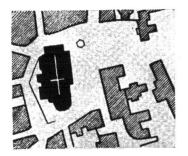

9

AUTUN

Saint Louis Plaza and Fountain of Saint Lazare

example of this. So also is the fountain of Rothenburg on the Tauber *(Figure 8)*.

In Italy, in front of the Palazzo Vecchio, on the Signoria of Florence, before the Palazzo Communale at Perugia, at the Palazzo Farnese in Rome, statues are located at the sides of streets and not on the axis of the principal structure of the public square. In France the fountain of Saint-Lazare at Autun *(Figure 9)* and the Fountain of the Innocents at Paris occupied the angle formed by the Rue aux Fers and the Rue Saint-Denis before 1786, instead of being aligned in the middle of the public square.

The location of the equestrian statue of Gattamelata by Donatello *(Figure 10)* in front of Saint Anthony of Padua is most instructive. First we may be astonished at its great variance from our rigid modern system, but it is quickly and strikingly seen that the monument in this place produces a

majestic effect. Finally we become convinced that removed to the center of the square its effect would be greatly diminished. We cease to wonder at its orientation and other locational advantages once this principle becomes familiar.

Thus to the ancient rule that prescribes the location of monuments at the edges of public squares may be added the principle followed during the Middle Ages, especially in cities of the north, according to ·which monuments and fountains were erected at points segregated from traffic. Now and then the two principles are put into practice simultaneously. They avoid common obstacles in seeking masterly artistic effects. Sometimes practical needs co-

10

PADUA:

Piazza del Santo

a. Column
b. Statue of Gattamelata

incide with artistic requisites, and this is understandable, for a traffic obstacle may also interfere with a good view. The location of monuments on the axes of monumental buildings or richly adorned portals should be avoided for it conceals worthwhile architecture from the eyes; and, re-

15

ciprocally, an excessively rich and ornate background is not appropriate for a monument. The ancient Egyptians understood this principle, for as Gattamelata and the little column stand beside the entrance to the Cathedral of Padua, the obelisks and the statues of the Pharaohs are aligned beside the temple doors. There is the entire secret that we refuse to decipher today.

The principle that we have just deduced applies not only to monuments and fountains, but to every type of construction, and especially to churches. Churches,

11

PADUA:

S. Giustina

which almost without exception occupy the center area of large sites, were not so located in former times. In Italy they are always set back with one or more sides against other buildings with which they form groups of open places that we shall now discuss.

The churches of Padua are classics in this respect. Only one side of San Giustina *(Figure 11)* is set back against other buildings. Two sides of San Antonio and the Carmine are so set back, while all of one side

with half of a second of the Jesuit church are so backed up. The bordering open space is quite irregular.

This is also to be seen at Verona where a further tendency to preserve a square of great dimensions before the prin-

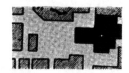

12

VERONA:

Cathedral Square

cipal entrance to the church *(Figure 12)* is observed; as in front of S. Fermo Maggiore *(Figure 13)*, S. Anastasia *(Figure 14)*, and others. Each of these places has its particular history and creates a vivid impression. The façades and portals of the churches which dominate them assume their full splendor. We rarely find an open place extending from the side of a church, as at S. Cita in Palermo *(Figure 15)*.

These few examples, in striking contrast to modern practices, are convincing enough to lead us into further study.

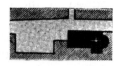

13

VERONA:

S. Fermo Maggiore

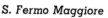

No city could serve as a better subject for this study than Rome with its numerous religious edifices. A study of them from the point of view of location yields a surprising result. Of the 255 churches, 41 are set back with one side against other buildings; 96 with two sides against other buildings; 110 with three sides against other buildings; 2 set in with four sides to other buildings; and 6 stand free of other buildings.

14

VERONA:

S. Anastasia

It should be said that among the last six mentioned there are two modern buildings, the Protestant and Anglican chapels, and that the four others are surrounded by narrow streets. This is equally contrary to the modern practice which superimposes the center of the church upon the center of the site. We can definitely conclude that in

15

PALERMO:

S. Cita

Rome churches are never entirely free standing, and the same may be said of all Italy, for the principle is in use just as much in Pavia as in Venice, where only the Cathedral stands free on all sides; Cremona; Milan (with the exception of the Cathedral); Reggio (including the Cathedral here); Fer-

are; and many other places. The type seen in Lucca *(Figure 16)* and Vicenza *(Figure 17)* recalls the principles that we deduced on the subject of locating monuments. It is even

16

LUCCA:

S. Michele

more appropriate for monumental buildings to be situated on the sides of public squares of average spaciousness, for in that way alone can they be best utilized and looked at from a convenient distance.

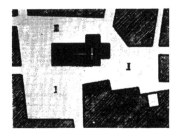

17

VICENZA

The case of the Cathedral of Brescia *(Figure 18)* is quite singular, but it is no exception to the rule, for the façade of the Cathedral serves as an enclosure for the open place. All of these observations indicate clearly that our modern systems are in direct opposition to established principles that were conscientiously observed in past epochs. We think it is impossible to place a new church anywhere except in the center of the site destined for it so that it will stand free on all sides, although this procedure is inconvenient and has few advantages. It detracts from the structure itself, for its potential effect cannot be concentrated but is scattered evenly around its circumference. Moreover, every organic relationship between the open place and its enclosure is made impossible, as all perspective effects require sufficient withdrawal. A cathedral

18

BRESCIA:

Cathedral Square showing old and new Cathedrals

requires a foreground to set off the majesty of its façade.

Location of a church in the middle of a site cannot even be defended in the name of the builder's interest, for it obliges him to extend, at great expense, all of the architectural features around the broad façades, the cornices, pedestals, and so on. In putting the building back with one or two sides against other buildings, the architect is spared all this expense, the free walls can be built of marble throughout, and there will still remain sufficient funds to embel-

lish them with statues. Thus we should not have these monotonous side faces running continuously around the building, the perfection of which cannot be appreciated from a single viewpoint. Furthermore, is it not often of advantage for a church to be joined to other buildings (cloisters or parsonages) in winter and bad weather? Besides, it is not only the building itself, but the public square as well, which suffers from the modern arrangement. Its name of place, square, or plaza is no longer any more than irony, for it is seldom more than a slightly widened street.

In spite of all these inconveniences, and in spite of all the precepts of the history of ecclesiastical architecture, modern churches are located throughout the world almost without exception in the center of their sites. We have lost all discernment.

Theaters, city halls, and numerous other structures are also victims of this erroneous conception. Perhaps we hopefully believe in the possibility of seeing all sides of a building at once, or it may be thought that an interesting building is especially distinguished if its walls stand entirely free. Nobody imagines that putting a void around a building prevents it from forming, with its environs, various diverse scenes. The lordly square masses of the Florentine palaces present a picturesque appearance when seen from the adjacent narrow passages. In this way these buildings acquire a double worth, for they present different appearances from the piazza and the vicolo.

Open Centers of Public Places

Modern taste is not satisfied with locating its own creations in the most unfavorable manner. It must also improve the works of the old masters by tearing them away from their surroundings. It does not hesitate to do so even when it is obvious that they have been designed to harmonize with the neighboring buildings, without which they would lose their worth. When a work of art is put in a place other than the one selected for it, part of its essential quality is taken away, and a great wrong is done to the artist who conceived it.

Performances of this kind are not rare. This rage for isolating everything is truly a modern sickness. R. Baumeister in his manual on city building even raises this to the status of a working principle. He writes, "Old buildings ought to be preserved, but we must, so to speak, peel them and preserve them." The object of this, then, is that by the transformation of surroundings the old buildings should be led to the midst of public places and in the axes of streets. This procedure is used everywhere and with special satisfaction in treating ancient city entrance portals. It is indeed a fine thing to have an isolated city gateway around which we may stroll instead of passing under its arches!

III

The Enclosed Character
of the Public Square

THE old practice of setting churches and palaces back against other buildings brings to mind the ancient forum and its unbroken frame of public buildings. In examining the public squares that came into being during the Middle Ages and the Renaissance, especially in Italy, it is seen that this pattern has been retained for ages by tradition. The old plazas produce a collective harmonious effect because they are uniformly enclosed. In fact, the public square owes its name to this characteristic in an expanse at the center of a city. It is true that we now use the term to indicate any parcel of land bounded by four streets on which all construction has been renounced.

That can satisfy the public health officer and the technician, but for the artist these few acres of ground are not yet a public square. Many things must be done to embellish the area to give it character and importance. For just as there are furnished and unfurnished rooms, we could speak of complete and incomplete squares. The essential thing of both room and square is the quality of enclosed space. It is the most essential condition of any artistic effect, although it is ignored by those who are now elaborating on city plans.

The ancients, on the contrary, employed the most diverse methods of fulfilling this condition under the most diverse circumstances. They were, it is true, supported by tradition and favored by the usual narrowness of streets and less active traffic movement. But it is precisely in cases where these aids were lacking that their talent and artistic feeling is displayed most conspicuously.

A few examples will assist in accounting for this. The following is the simplest. Directly facing a monumental building a large gap was made in a mass of masonry, and the square thus created, com-

19

BRESCIA:

San Giovanni

pletely surrounded by buildings, produced a happy effect. Such is the Piazza S. Giovanni at Brescia *(Figure 19)*. Often a second street opens on to a small square, in which case care is taken to avoid an excessive breach in the border, so that the principal building will remain well enclosed. The methods used by the ancients to accomplish this were so greatly varied that chance alone could not have guided them. Undoubtedly they were often assisted by circumstance, but they also knew how to use circumstances admirably.

Today in such cases all obstructions would be taken down and large breaches in the border of the public place would be opened, as is done when we decide to "modernize" a city. Ancient streets would be found to open on the square in a manner precisely contrary to the methods of modern city builders, and mere chance would not account for this. Today the practice is to join two streets that intersect at right angles at each corner of the square, probably to enlarge as much as possible the opening made in the enclosure and to destroy every impression of cohesion. Formerly the procedure was entirely different. There was an effort to have only one street at each angle of the square. If a second artery was needed in a direction at right angles to the first, it was designed to terminate at a sufficient distance from the square to remain out of view from the square. And better still, the three or four streets which came in at the corners each ran in a different direction. This interesting arrangement was reproduced so frequently, and more or less completely, that it can be considered as one of the conscious or subconscious principles of ancient city building.

Careful study shows that there are many advantages to an arrangement of street openings in the form of turbine arms. From any part of the square there is but one exit on the streets opening into it, and the enclosure of buildings is not broken. It even

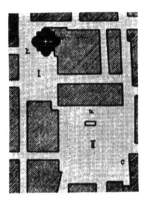

20

PARMA:

a. Pal. del Commune
b. Madonna della Steccata
c. Pal. della Podesteria
I. Piazza d. Steccata
II. Piazza Grande

seems to enclose the square completely, for the buildings set at an angle conceal each other, thanks to perspective, and unsightly impressions which might be made by openings are avoided. The secret of this is in having streets enter the square at right angles to the visual lines instead of parallel to them. Joiners and carpenters have fol-

21

RAVENNA:

Cathedral Square

lowed this principle since the Middle Ages when, with subtle art, they sought to make

21

joints of wood and stone inconspicuous if not invisible.

The Cathedral Square at Ravenna *(Figure 21)* shows the purest type of the arrangement just described. The square of Pistoia *(Figure 22)* is in the same manner; as is the Piazza S. Pietro at Mantua *(Figure 23)*, and the Piazza Grande at Parma *(Figure 20)*. It is a little more difficult to recognize the

22

PISTOIA:

Cathedral Square

a. Cathedral
b. Bapistry
c. Residence
d. Palais de la Commune
e. Palais du Podestat

principle in the Signoria of Florence *(Figure 24)*. The principal streets conform to the rule. The narrow strip of land of about a yard's width (at the side of the Loggia dei Lanzi) is much less noticeable in reality than it is on the map.

The ancients had recourse to still other means of closing in their squares. Often they broke the infinite perspective of a street by a monumental portal or by several arcades of which the size and number were determined by the intensity of traffic circulation. This splendid architectural pattern has almost entirely disappeared, or, more accurately, it has been suppressed. Again Florence gives us one of the best examples in the portico of the Uffizi with its view of the Arno in the distance. Every Ital-

ian city of average importance has its portico, and this is also true north of the Alps. We mention only the Langasser Thor at Danzig, the entrance portal of the City Hall and Chancellery at Bruges, the Kerkboog at Nimeguen, the great Bell Tower at Rouen, the monumental Portals of Nancy, and the windows of the Louvre.

More or less ornate portals like those that simply but effectively frame the Piazza dei Signoria at Verona *(Figure 25)* are to be found in all the royal residences, in the chateaux and city halls, and they are used as much for vehicular traffic as by pedestrians. While ancient architects used this pattern wherever possible with infinite variations, our modern builders seem to ignore its existence. Let us recall, to demonstrate again the persistence of ancient tradi-

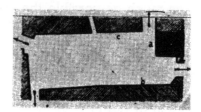

23

MANTUA: Piazza S. Pietro

a. S. Pietro   b. Pal. Reale

c. P. Vescovile

tions, that at Pompeii, too, there is an *Arc de Triomphe* at the entrance to the Forum.

Columns were used with porticos to form enclosures for public squares. Saint Peter's in Rome is the best example of this. In more modest proportions there is the hemicycle of the Place de la Carrière at Nancy. Sometimes portico and columns are combined as in the Cathedral Square at Salzburg. At S. Maria Novella in Florence the colonnade is replaced by a wall of rich architectural embellishment. At times public squares are completely surrounded by

24

FLORENCE:

Piazza della Signoria

high walls opened by simple or monumental portals, as at the ancient episcopal residence of Bamberg (1591), at the City Hall of Altenbourg (1562-1564), at the old university of Fribourg-en-Brusgau, and other places.

Arcades were used to embellish monumental buildings more frequently in former times than at present, either on the higher stories, as in the City Halls of Halle (1548) and Cologne (1568), or on the ground level. Among the numerous examples, we call attention to arcades of the city halls of Paderborn, Ypres (1621-1622), Amsterdam, Lübeck, the Cloth Market at Brunswick, the City Hall at Brigue; arcades of market places, as at Münster and Bologna, or like the Portico dei Servi in the latter City. Let us recall also the beautiful portico of the Palazzo Podesta at Bologna, and at Brescia the superb arcade of Monte Vecchio, the fine

25

VERONA: Piazza dei Signori

23

loggias of Udine and of San Annunziata at Florence. And finally, the arcade pattern was used in a thousand ways in the architecture of courts, cloisters, and cemeteries.

All of these above mentioned architectural forms in former times made up a complete system of enclosing public squares. Today there is a contrary tendency to open them on all sides. It is easy to describe the results that have come about. It has tended to destroy completely the old public squares. Wherever these openings have been made the cohesive effect of the square has been completely nullified.

IV

The Form and Expanse
of Public Squares

WE can distinguish between two kinds of public squares, those of depth and those of expanse. This classification has only a relative value, however, because it depends on the position of the observer and the direction in which he is looking. Thus, one square could have both forms at the same time, depending upon the observer's position with respect to a building, at the principal side or at one of the lesser sides of the square. In general, the character of a square is determined by one building of special importance.

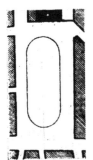

26

FLORENCE:

S. Croce

For example, the Piazza di S. Croce at Florence *(Figure 26)* is rather deep, because it is usually looked at while facing the church. Its bulk and its monuments are

arranged to produce their best effect in a given direction. We readily see that a square having depth makes a favorable impression only when the dominant building is of rather slender form, as is the case with most churches. If the square extends from a building of exceptional breadth its contours should be modified accordingly.

If, then, church squares should generally be deep, the squares of city halls ought to be expansive. The position of monuments in either case should be determined by the form of the public square. The Piazza Reale at Modena *(Figure 27)* is an example

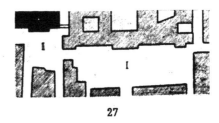

27

MODENA:

I. Piazza Reale   II. P. di S. Dominico

of a well arranged expansive square, in form as well as in dimensions. The adjoining Piazza di S. Dominico is deep. Moreover, the manner in which the different streets open into the square is noteworthy. Everything is arranged to present a perfect setting. The street in front of the church does not detract from the general effect by breaking the enclosure, since it runs perpendicularly to the direction of the observer's view. Neither do the two streets opening in the direction of the façade have a disturbing effect, for the observer turns his back on them in looking at the church. The projecting left wing of the chateau is not the work of pure chance. It serves to confine the view within the church square and to make a definite separation between the two squares.

The contrast between these two adjoining squares is striking. The effect of one is intensified by the opposing effect of the other. One is large, the other small; one expansive, the other deep; one is dominated by a palace, the other by a church.

It is truly a delight for the sensitive observer to analyze such a plan and to find the explanation for its wonderful effect. Like all true works of art, it continually reveals new beauties and further reason for admiring the methods and the resourcefulness of the ancient city builders. They had frequent occasion to find answers to difficult problems, for they took full account of contemporary necessities. That is why we seldom find "pure types" in their work, which developed slowly with the inspiration of a sound tradition.

It is difficult to determine the exact relationship that ought to exist between the magnitude of a square and the buildings which enclose it, but clearly it should be an harmonious balance. An excessively small square is worthless for a monumental structure. A square that is too big is even worse, for it will have the effect of reducing its dimensions, however colossal they may actually be. This has been observed thousands of times at Saint Peter's in Rome.

It is a delusion to think that the feeling of magnitude created by a square increases indefinitely with extensions of its size. We have already learned by experience in some places that continual expansion does not produce proportionate increases in impressiveness. It has been observed that the intensity of sound produced by a men's choir is increased at once by voices that are added to it, but there is a point at which the maximum effect is reached and at which the addition of more singers ceases to improve it. (This point is reached with 400 singers). This seems to be applicable to the impression of magnitude that can be created by certain public squares. If a narrow strip of a few yards is added to a small square the result is quite sensible and usually advantageous, but if the square is already large this increase is scarcely noticed, for the relative proportions of square and surrounding buildings remain about the same. Great esplanades are no longer found in modern cities except in the form of recreational areas. They can scarcely be considered as forming public squares since the buildings around them are like country houses in the open, or like villages seen from a distance.

The Form and Expanse of Public Squares

Some places of this type are the Champ de Mars at Paris, the Campo di Marte at Venice, the Piazza d'Armi at Trieste, and the Piazza d'Armi at Turin. Although they do not come within the scope of our study, we mention them here because they have frequently been copied in the interior of cities with badly proportioned dimensions. Great buildings around them are reduced in appearance to ordinary rank, for in architecture the relationship of proportion plays a greater role than absolute size. Statues of dwarfs that are six feet or more in height may be seen in public gardens. They stand in contrast to statuettes of Hercules of Tom Thumb size. Thus the greatest of the gods is made a dwarf, and the smallest of men becomes heroic.

The person who is interested in city building should study the dimensions of some of the smaller squares and of a large square of his own city. It will convince him that the feeling of magnitude that they produce is often out of proportion to their actual dimensions. Above all it is important to achieve good relative proportion between the dimensions of a square and the enclosing buildings. This relationship, like all precepts of art, is difficult to establish precisely, for it must frequently submit to wide variations. A glance at the map of any great city demonstrates this. It is much easier to determine the proportions of a column and its entablature. It would be desirable to determine the relationship within a definite approximation, especially now when plans for city expansion are dashed off according to the whims of the draftsman and not gradually in accordance with the needs of the time. To assist in solving this important problem we have prepared the plans which accompany this study as far as possible on a common scale. It will be asserted that the variety of methods employed in past ages indicates almost arbitrary practice. However, it is possible to draw from an examination of them the following principles, which, in spite of platitudinous appearance, are far from being observed today.

1. The principal squares of large cities are larger than those of small cities.
2. In each city some principal public squares have expansive dimensions, while others must remain within confined limits.
3. The dimensions of public squares also depend on the importance of the principal buildings which dominate them; or, put another way, the height of the principal building, measured from the ground to the cornice, should be in proportion to the dimension of the public square measured perpendicularly in the direction of the principal façade. In public squares of depth the height of the façade of the church should be compared with the depth of the square. In public squares of expanse the height of the façade of the palace or public building should be compared with the breadth of the square.

Experience shows that the minimum dimension of a square ought to be equal to the height of the principal building in it, and that its maximum dimension ought not to exceed twice that height unless the form, the purpose, and the design of the building will support greater dimensions. Buildings of medium height can be built on large public squares if, thanks to the few stories and massive architecture, they can be developed better in breadth.

It is also important to consider the relationship that should exist between the length and breadth of a public square. In this, exact rules are of little worth, for the problem is not one of obtaining a good result on paper only but in reality as well. But the actual effect will depend largely on the position of the observer, and it may be said in passing that it is quite difficult to make accurate estimates of distance; and, too, we have but an imperfect perception of the relationship between length and breadth of a plaza. Let us say then only that public squares that are actually square are few in number and unattractive; that excessively elongated "squares" (where length is more than three times the width) have a scarcely better appearance. Expansive squares, in general, have much greater discrepancies between their two dimensions than squares which have depth. However, that depends on circumstances. The streets opening on to the square must also be considered. Narrow little streets of the old cities require squares of only modest dimensions, while today vast squares are needed to accommodate our streets of great width. Modern streets of medium width (from 50 to 100 feet) would have been wide enough in past ages to form one of the sides of a typical, well-enclosed church square. Of course, that would only have been made possible by clever design and by the narrow width of old streets (from 6½ to 26 feet). What should be the dimensions of an adequate and well proportioned square, located on a street of from 150 to 200 feet wide? The Ringstrasse at Vienna is 186 feet wide; the Esplanade at Hamburg, 150; the Linden at Berlin, 190. Such dimensions are not even attained by the Piazza di San Marco at Venice, and there is still the Avenue des Champs-Elysees at Paris which is 465 feet wide. The average dimensions of the great squares of the old cities are 465 by 190 feet.

There can be observed a modern nervous sickness, the fear of squares. Many people suffer from it. They become ill in crossing a wide square. Even great men moulded in bronze or sculptured in stone have been struck by this disease on their monumental pedestals. They prefer, as we have seen, to remain in the old small squares rather than venture into vast deserted spaces. How large should statues on large squares be? At least two or three times human stature. We have said that the fear of squares is an entirely modern malady, and understandably so, since the old, small squares gave a feeling of comfortable snugness. It is only within our own memory that they have taken on enormous proportions, for the impression of vastness that disturbs us surpasses actual magnitude. On the other hand, we quickly forget the large squares we have crossed, and the impression of them that is retained in the memory keeps them of a size that nullifies their artistic worth. Their most unfortunate influence is brought to bear on the enclosing buildings, which can never be large enough. Even if the architect exhausts every re-

source of his art and heaps mass upon mass surpassing all previous performances, the effect never fulfills the artistic and material requirements of his medium.

R. Baumeister, in the work previously referred to, criticizes expansive squares as having no hygienic value, as being sources of heat and dust, and as traffic obstructions. Nevertheless, we are surpassing ourselves today in planning such squares, and with a certain logic, for at least they correspond to our boundless streets.

28

VICENZA:

Piazza dei Signori

V

The Irregularity of Ancient Public Squares

ECHNICIANS of today take more trouble than is necessary to create interminable rectangular streets and public squares of impeccable symmetry. These efforts seem misdirected to those who are interested in good city appearance. Our forebears had ideas on this subject quite different to ours. Here is some evidence of it: the Piazza dei Eremitani and the Piazza del Duomo at Padua *(Figure 29)*, the Cathedral Square at Syracuse *(Figure 31)*, and the Piazza S. Francesco at Palermo *(Figure 30)*.

29

PADUA:

Cathedral and Cathedral Square

The typical irregularity of these old squares indicates their gradual historical development. We are rarely mistaken in attributing the existence of these windings to practical causes — the presence of a canal, the lines of an old roadway, or the form of a building. Everyone knows from personal experience that these disruptions in symmetry are not unsightly. On the contrary, they arouse our interest as much as

they appear natural, and preserve a picturesque character. Few people, however, understand why irregularity can avoid giving an unpleasant appearance. We must study a map to understand it. Any city can

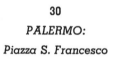

30

PALERMO:

Piazza S. Francesco

offer a good example of this, for the eye is inclined to overlook slight irregularities and is incapable of evaluating angles. We are willing to see more regularity in forms than actually exists.

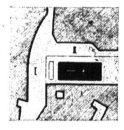

31

SYRACUSE:

I. Piazza del Duomo
II. Piazza Minerva

Whoever studies a map of his own city can be convinced that violent irregularities, shown on the map, do not in the least seem to be striking irregularities when seen on the ground. The celebrated Piazza d'Erbe at Verona *(Figure 32)* is known to nearly everybody from engravings if not from experience, but undoubtedly there are few who have observed the irregular shape

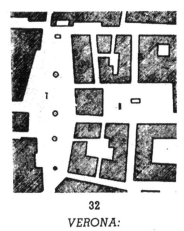

32

VERONA:

I. Piazza d'Erbe   II. Piazza dei Signori

of this square. That is not surprising, for nothing is more difficult than to recompose the plan of a place from a perspective view,

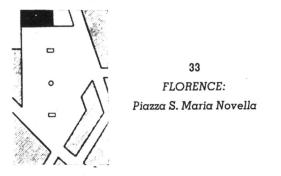

33

FLORENCE:

Piazza S. Maria Novella

and especially so from memory. While we are looking at an impressive sight it does not occur to us to analyze structural details.

The difference between a graphic representation and an actual view of the Piazza S. Maria Novella at Florence *(Figure 33)* is equally surprising. In fact, the square has five sides, but, in the memory of many travelers, it has only four. For on the ground only three sides of it can be seen at one time, and the angle formed by the two other sides is always behind the observer's back. Furthermore, we are easily mistaken in calculat-

32A

VERONA: Piazza Erbe

ing by sight the angle formed by these two sides. Perspective makes this calculation difficult even for engineers if they use only their eyes. This is truly a square of surprises, for in it we are subjected to so many varied optical illusions. It is a far cry indeed from the rigorous symmetry so dear to modern city builders.

It is strange that the slightest irregularity in modern city plans upsets us, although those of ancient public squares do not have a displeasing appearance. In fact, their irregularities are such that they are seen only on paper. On the ground they escape us. The ancients did not conceive their plans on drawing boards. Their buildings rose bit by bit *in natura*. Thus they were readily governed by that which struck the eye in reality. They did not stop to correct

S. Pietro alle scale   S. Vigilio

V. d. Abbadia   S. Maria di Provenzano

34

SIENNA

defects in symmetry that were evident only on paper. The various squares of Sienna offer proof of this *(Figure 34)*.

In all of these examples we can clearly see the tendency to create squares having depth in front of church façades to provide a good view for important build-ings. The observer facing the edifice cannot see the most irregular sides of the square, for his back is to them. Thus the square avoids an excessively broken appearance and forms a well proportioned whole.

We know how little symmetry and absolute geometrical regularity contributed to the picturesque beauty of medieval castles. In spite of their tormented structures, these old castles achieved an harmonious impression because their architecture clearly explained what was in them. Each individual structural mass has a kind of counterbalance which assures an overall equilibrium, boldly conceived and composed of patterns that were varied but not confusing. There is much of this in the art of building cities. Here the liberty of the artist is a still greater factor, for the realm of applied artistic resources is much vaster, and the methods at his disposal are so numerous that they may all be used without infringing on each other. Why then should we be content with the stiff regularity, the useless symmetry, and the tiresome uniformity of modern city plans? In parts of old country houses and in the architecture of castles we perceive a certain picturesque abandon. Why must the straightedge and the compass be the all powerful masters of city building?

The notion of symmetry is propagating itself today like the spread of an epidemic. The least cultivated are familiar with it, and each one feels called upon to have his say about the involved artistic matters that concern the building of cities, for each thinks he has at his finger tips the single criterion—symmetry. Although this is a Greek word, its ancient meaning was quite different from its present meaning.

The notion of identical figures to the right and left of an axis was not the basis of any theory in ancient times. Whoever has taken the trouble to search out the meaning of the word "symmetry" in Greek and Latin literature knows that it means something that cannot be expressed in a single word today. Even Vitruvius had to translate it by paraphrase. He says (I, 2, 4): *Item symmetria est ex ipsius operis membris conveniens consensus ex partibusque separatis ad universae figurae speciem ratae partis responsus.** That is why his terminology is always variable, except when he deliberately adopts the Greek term. At times he substitutes for it *proportio*, which is a little more exact interpretation, but he does not like to use this term for he says himself that symmetry results from *proportio quae graec* **analogia** *dicitur*** (III, 1, 1). In short, proportion and symmetry were the same to the ancients. The sole difference between the two is that in architecture proportion is simply a relationship agreeable to the eye, like the relationship between the diameter and height of a column, while symmetry is the same relationship expressed in numbers. This meaning remained valid throughout the Middle Ages.

When Gothic masters began to form architectural patterns and became more concerned with the axes of symmetry in the modern sense of the term, the notion of similarity of figures to the left and right of a principal line was established in theory. An ancient name, with its meaning altered, was given to this idea. Writers of the Renaissance were using it in this sense. Since then, the axes of symmetry have become continually more frequent in plans for buildings, as they have in plans for cities. Aided by this alone, the modern architect undertakes to perform all the tasks that are thrust on him. Our self-styled esthetic principles of building are at hand to prove the deficiency of this unfortunate principle. Everybody insists that a rule governing the building of cities cannot completely ignore the laws of beauty, but, since the problem is one of moving from theory to practice, initial enthusiasm gives way to utter confusion. The mouse brought forth by the mountain is universal, inevitable, indisputable, essential *symmetry!* Thus a syrupy law of 1864 sought to satisfy the artistic requirements of the country by enjoining the architects to avoid everything that "could offend symmetry and morality" in the design of façades. It remains to be learned which of the two offenses was considered the graver.

In modern cities irregularity in plan is unsuccessful because it has been created

---

*Symmetry also is the appropriate harmony arising out of the details of the work itself; the correspondence of each given detail among the separate details to the form of the design as a whole. (Granger Translation)
**Proportion, which in Greek is called *analogia*.

artificially with the straightedge. It most often takes the form of triangular public places—the fatal dregs of drawing board plotting. They nearly always have a bad effect. There is no illusion to the eye, for the clashing intersection of building lines are always in view. The sole means of remedying the defects of such places would be to make each side irregular in itself. That would bring about numerous recesses, partially symmetrical, and open spaces removed from traffic where monuments and statues might be advantageously situated. Unfortunately, that is impossible today, for

since each of the three sides of a triangular "square" is rigorously straight, all efforts toward pleasing treatment are in vain. From this springs the legend of regular and irregular squares which holds that the first class are beautiful and suitable for monuments located, it is needless to say, in the geometrical center. If we limit ourselves to modern squares, this assertion is true, but when we begin to examine those of past epochs we see that irregular squares can be more readily adorned with statues and monuments, for they do not lack suitable places for them.

VI

W E have already had occasion in our study to compare two squares located close together, and our illustrations have shown numerous other examples of similar groupings. They are so frequent, especially in Italy, that cities having the principal buildings grouped about a single square are rather exceptional. This is a result of the old practice of closing the frame of the square and setting churches and palaces back against other buildings.

Let us study the plan of Modena (*Figure 35*). The Piazza Grande is evidently intended to set off the lateral façade of the church. It is also of rather elongated shape and extends beyond the vault. This might be expressed theoretically by saying that a façade square and a vault square are joined together. The squares I and II are, on the contrary, quite distinct from each other. The Piazza Grande makes a complete entity by itself, and the Piazza Torre likewise has its individual character. Its purpose is to open up a perspective on the church tower, which thus produces its entire effect. Moreover, Square I, which commands the principal façade, is deep, conforming to the rule. The street opening there in the direction of the portal does not interfere with the harmony of the whole. At Lucca the Piazza

Grande and the double square at the Cathedral, with one part in front of the church and the other at its side, establish a comparable rule. These examples, which could be multiplied indefinitely, demonstrate that the different façades of buildings have de-

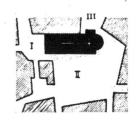

35

MODENA:

I. Piazza delle Legna
II. Piazza Grande
III. Piazza Torre

termined the form of the corresponding public squares in order to produce a fine work. In fact, it is not likely that two or three squares would have been created unless the various façades of a church could be readily adapted to it afterward. In any case, it is certain that this combination brings out all the beauties of a monumental building. We can scarcely ask for more than three squares and three different views, each forming an harmonious whole, around a single church.

This is new evidence of the wisdom of the ancients who, with a minimum of material resources, knew how to achieve great effects. It might almost be said that their procedures constitute a method for the greatest utilization of monumental buildings. In fact, each remarkable façade has a square to itself, and reciprocally, each square has its marble façade. That, too, has its importance, for those superb stone elevations, so desirable for giving a square enough character to save it from banality, are not found just everywhere.

This cleverly refined method can no longer be used, since its application requires the existence of well enclosed squares and buildings set back against other structures—two practices equally foreign to the style of the times, which prefers open breaches everywhere.

36

PERUGIA:

I. Piazza del Duomo
II. Piazza dei Papa
a. Palazzo communale

But let us return to the old masters. At Perugia the Piazza di S. Lorenzo *(Figure 36)* separates the Cathedral from the Palazzo Communale. It is, then, both a cathedral square and a town hall square. Square III is given over to the cathedral. At Vicenza the Basilica of Palladio *(Figure 38)* is surrounded by two squares, each of which has its special character. Similarly, the Signoria at Florence *(Figure 24)* also has its sec-

ondary square in the Portico of the Uffizi. From an architectural point of view this Signoria is the most remarkable square in the world. Every resource of the city building art has made its contribution here — the

37

MANTUA:

S. Andrea

I. Piazza d'Erbe

shape and dimensions of the square, contrasting with those of the adjoining square; the manner in which streets open; the location of fountains and monuments; all of this is admirably studied. Yet, it required an unequaled quantity of labor. Several generations of able artists used centuries in transforming this site, of no special excellence in itself, into a masterpiece of architecture. We never tire of this spectacle, which is as pleasingly effective as the means of fabricating it are inconspicuous.

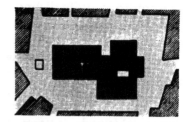

38

VICENZA:

Piazza of the Signori at the Basilica of Palladio

Venice also has a combination of squares that are remarkable in every way, the Piazza di S. Marco (I) and the Piazzetta

(II) *(Figure 39. See also frontispiece and Figure 40).* The first is a square having depth with respect to Saint Marks and an expansive square with respect to the Procuraties. Similarly, the second is expansive with respect to the palace of the Doges and, primarily, deep with respect to the superb scene formed by the Grand Canal with the Campanile S. Giorgio Maggiore in the distance. There is a third small square before the lateral façade of Saint Marks. There is

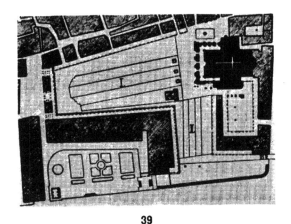

39

VENICE:

I. P. S. Marco   II. Piazzetta

such an expanse of beauty here that no painter has ever conceived an architectural background more perfect than its setting. No theater ever created a more sublime tableau than the spectacle to be enjoyed at Venice. It is truly the seat of a great power, a power of spirit, of art, and of industry which has gathered the treasures of the world upon its vessels, which has thrust its supremacy over all the seas, and which has possessed its accumulated riches on this spot of the globe. The imagination of a Titian or of a Paul Veronese could not conceive of picture cities, in their backgrounds for great festival scenes, more splendid than these.

This unequaled grandeur assuredly was attained through extraordinary means: the effect of the sea, the great number of buildings embellished with sculpture, the magnificent coloring of Saint Marks, and the towering Campanile. But the exceptional effect of this assembly of marvels is due largely to skillful arrangement. We may be quite certain that these works of art would lose much of their value if they were located haphazardly by means of the compass and straightedge according to the modern system. Imagine Saint Marks isolated from its surroundings and transplanted to the center of a gigantic modern square; or the Procuraties, the library, and the Campanile, instead of being closely grouped, spread out over a wide area, and bordered by a 200 foot wide boulevard. What a nightmare for an artist! The masterpiece would thus be reduced to nothing. The splendor of buildings alone is not enough to form a magnificent whole if the general arrangement of the square is not carefully worked out. The shape of St. Mark's Plaza, and of the squares that are subordinate to it, conforms to every principle that we have thus far discussed. We should note especially the location of the Campanile, which, rising between the two squares, seems to stand guard.

What an impression is made by several grouped squares on the person who goes from one to the other! The eye encounters a new scene every instant, and we feel an infinite variety of impressions. This may be observed in photographs of St. Mark's and of the Signoria of Florence.

There are more than a dozen popular views of each square, taken from various points. Each one presents a different picture, so much so that it is sometimes difficult to believe that they are all views of the same place. When we examine a modern square of strict right angle design, we can get only two or three views of different quality, for in general they express no artistic feeling. They are only surfaces of so much area.

40

VENICE: La Piazzetta

VII

Arrangement of Public Squares
in Northern Europe

THUS far, most of our illustrations have been drawn from Italian cities of renowned classic beauty. It may be questioned, however, whether we in the north of Europe have been able to reproduce them. Climate, living habits, types of dwellings, and building methods are essentially different here. Does it not follow, then, that streets and squares must also be different? Tremendous changes that have come about make it impossible for us to follow ancient models. Even if we returned to polytheism we could not now build five or six or more temples around a single forum as the ancients did. Similarly, our houses are built quite differently from theirs. They have their origin in the covered "halle" of the northern countries with its numerous windows that open onto thoroughfares. Thus we must have different kinds of squares and streets to satisfy our needs.

During the Middle Ages and the Renaissance the influence of the German house changed the character of dwellings even in Italy, so that the "cortile" with its open arcade soon became the sole vestige of the ancient house. In the same way the ancient type of forum disappeared, for the people of Italy adopted a new manner of living more like that of other peoples of Europe. The difference that exists between buildings of the Renaissance and those of antiquity, as much in Italy as in the North, is much greater than the difference between German Gothic and Italian Gothic, or between German Renaissance and Italian Renaissance.

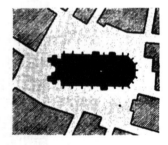

41

FREIBURG:

Cathedral Square

Perhaps the greatest contrast between Italian practices and those of the northern countries is in the building of churches and church plazas. In the North, cathedrals are frequently isolated, if not in the center of a square, at least in a way that separates them from other buildings by a complete border of street area. In large cities that is done only with one or two principal churches, for here also we find many churches of lesser importance set back against other structures. The usual explanation of this isolation of cathedrals is the previous existence of a cemetery in the midst of which a chapel was built, as may still be seen in many villages. For examples of this practice we may refer to the Cathedral Square of Freiburg *(Figure 41)*, the Frauenkirche at Munich *(Figure 42)*, the Cathedral of Ulm *(Figure 43)*, Jakobskirche at Stettin *(Figure 44)*, St. Stephans at Vienna, and numerous others. Where there is no cemetery to require this kind of isolation, the more desirable placement of churches against other structures is followed. This is

42

MUNICH:

Frauenplatz

nearly always the case with respect to Renaissance and Baroque churches since the practice of locating cemeteries in the centers of cities was not followed in those times.

But such isolation of buildings is only moderate, especially in the case of Gothic churches, and even that differs from modern practice. The normal placing of a Gothic cathedral is such that houses border both sides and the choir, with but slight separation from the sanctuary by a narrow passage-way. There is usually a large plaza in front of the main portal to set off the façade and towers. This arrangement is undoubtedly the most favorable to Gothic con-

struction. It provides a view from the front over the façade and mighty towers exactly as needed to give expression. to the gran-

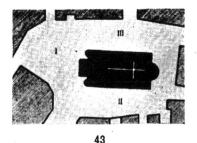

43

ULM:

I. Cathedral Square   II. Upper Churchyard
III. Lower Churchyard

diose motif of the building. The value of providing a further view of the soaring structure from vastly wider streets directly opposite the main portal is shown to be questionable wherever it is even half-way approached. A view of the Strassburg Cathedral from the narrow street opening

44

STETTIN:

Jakobi-Kirchhof

on to the main portal shows the excellence of this arrangement *(Figure 45)*. A similar effect is attempted in the cases of the Sebalduskirche and the Lorenzokirche at

45
STRASSBURG: *Münster*

Nuremburg as far as the narrow, crooked streets of the old city permit it.

However, the lateral façade of a Gothic church should be treated differently. It is all movement, descending from the lofty towers to the low chapel of the choir. The symmetrical center of the nave sides is not actually in the middle of them. The exterior but translates the interior essence of the building, and this is irreconcilable with a wide prospect of it from a great distance. Even on paper, in representing the lateral façade of a church with its towers, the entire upper part of the towers must be omitted if a design of good proportion is to be produced. This suggests that the old Gothic churches were so snugly enclosed, with free access only to the main portal, entirely for their own advantage. Access to the principal portal naturally meets the need of crowds moving toward the building, the entry of a procession, and so on. A venerable Gothic church placed in the midst of a vast drill place, it is readily seen, would have its essential quality and its powerful effect put at naught. This may be observed in the free placement of Cologne cathedral from the point of view of one approaching it, and especially in the small Votive Church at Vienna in a larger plaza.

If St. Stephan's at Vienna were placed on the empty vastness of the Votive Church Plaza it would lose its present mysterious effect, while the glorious Votive Church, if it could be put on the site of the Strassburg Cathedral or of Notre Dame of Paris, would make a much stronger impression than it can in its present unfavorable surroundings.

Thus the old principle of building churches against other buildings has been followed in the north of Europe with some difference in application. Of the twelve churches and Cathedral in Strassburg, only one is free-standing. Similarly, all of the old churches in Mainz, including the Cathedral, are built against other structures. The same is true of Bamberg, Frankfurt-am-Main, and other cities. While the practice is not universal, most of the old churches are built in this manner. Isolation of church buildings in the north is an exception to the general rule, and wherever it exists it contains its explanation (the presence of an ancient cemetery). Otherwise the partially rounded form of church plazas, as seen in northern German cities like Danzig, would be inexplicable.

46

FRANKFURT am Main

*St. Pauls
and Plaza*

This exception does not invalidate the artistic value of the ancient building principle, for the old churches are never found in the middle of their squares. Their geometric centers never coincide with those of their squares. The pedantic, futile, modern practice that makes excessive use of the straightedge and compass succeeds only in reducing the effect of buildings and squares to the minimum at one fell blow. There are numerous examples, like St. Paul's at Frankfurt-am-Main *(See Figures 46-50)*, to show how differently our predecessors thought of this.

47

CONSTANCE:

St. Stephans and its Plaza

Although St. Paul's is completely free-standing, it is so cleverly drawn back into the end enclosure of the square that it seems to be built into the architectural mass that surrounds it. St. Stephan's at Constance has a similar placement and, in addition, two distinctly separated church squares. Essen-

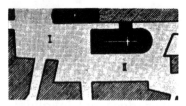

48

REGENSBURG:

I. Cathedral Square
II. Cathedral Street

tially the same arrangement may be observed in the Cathedral Square at Regensburg, where the square takes the form of depth (within the terms of our previous discussion) and the wide Cathedral Street, dominated by the lateral façade of the

church, takes an expansive form. The cathedrals of Constance and Schwerin follow the Italian principle of using three free sides of a monumental building to form separate and distinct plazas.

It is scarcely necessary to go further in showing that the old plazas of the north-

49

CONSTANCE:

The Cathedral with its Plazas

ern countries differ from the Italian only in form and size, and that they have a common irregularity. Varied possibilities in arrangement are to be observed in the location of the Cathedral of Wurzburg *(Figure 51)* and

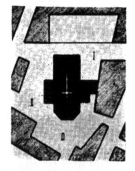

50

SCHWERIN:

The Cathedral

the Church of St. Nicholas at Kiel *(Figure 52)* as well as in the three plazas of the Royal Theater at Copenhagen *(Figure 53)*.

The value of old building principles

is even more evident in the market places and city hall squares than it is in church plazas. Here again we find conformity to the general practice of grouping architectural masses around open space. Perhaps a few examples can suffice to indicate the variety in this general type.

51

WURZBURG:

a. Cathedral
b. New Church
I. Parade Plaza
II. Church Plaza
III. Cathedral Plaza

An interesting combination of buildings and squares may be seen at Brunswick (*Figure 54*), where St. Martin's Church has a square of depth before its principal façade and a square of expanse along its lateral façade, while the old City Hall, built back against other structures, dominates the

52

KIEL:

St. Nicholas Church

a. City Hall

Market Place. Scorning these fine models, the new City Hall has been built standing free on a remote site with no structural relationship to other buildings. The Clothworkers Hall is surrounded by plazas appropriate to the façades which dominate them

—squares of depth adjoining the narrow sides, and squares of expanse extending from the lateral walls. Thus the ensemble is composed of closely related parts in a manner that enhances the effect of each plaza and building.

53

COPENHAGEN:

a. Royal Theater

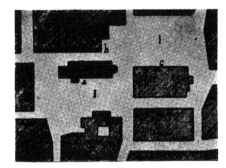

54

BRUNSWICK:

a. St. Martins Church
b. Old City Hall
c. Cloth-Hall
I. Market Square

A similar harmonious effect has been produced at Stettin by the location of the City Hall (*Figure 55*) with respect to the surrounding open space. Two sides of the City

Hall at Cologne *(Figure 56)* are built into other structures, but each end of the building commands a separate and distinct public square. The old City Hall of Hannover *(Figure 57)* stands at the edge of the Market Square, and again at Lübeck the City Hall

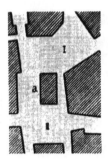

55

STETTIN:

a. City Hall

(Figure 58) is placed between the Market Place and the Cathedral Plaza so that it helps form the enclosure of each. We might go on indefinitely listing examples of this kind.

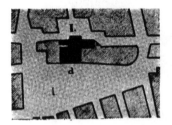

56

COLOGNE

a. City Hall
I. Old Market

In some of them we find that streets do not open on to squares according to the old principles. Circumstance usually accounts for this, but, even so, the poorest arrangements we find result in more coherent architectural ensembles than the man-

gled, excessively opened public squares of modern times. The winding and crooked streets at least made for appreciable perspectives superior to parallels vanishing at infinity.

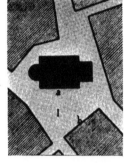

57

HANNOVER:

a. St. Martins Church
b. Old City Hall
I. Market Square

Obviously the model of the ancient forum was followed by the builders of northern cities. They produced original results out of old principles by choosing the most natural solutions to their practical prob-

58

LUBECK:

a. Cathedral
c. City Hall
I. Market Square

lems. This simplified matters for them, for they undertook to judge the effect of their projected buildings on the particular sites and in the natural settings intended for them, and their determinations were made accordingly. Modern architects often design structures for sites that they have never seen. That inevitably leads to banal work, for the building conceived for construction on just any site goes up, through the workings of a perverse fate, in the midst of an empty expanse without the slightest correlation to its surroundings, and without balance between its height and that of neighboring structures.

Our era is marked by the mass production of buildings stamped out according to some accepted standard. The old builders, on the contrary, knew how to place their most important structures around a plaza in a way that could give character to an entire city despite the fact that the direct effect of such groupings was necessarily exercised in a single place. Figure 59 shows

59

BREMEN:

I. Cathedral Yard
II. Market Square with
   Statue of Roland
a. Cathedral
b. City Hall
   and Treasury
c. Frauenkirche

the placement of buildings around the Town Hall of Bremen. What is it that harmonizes all of the monumental construction amassed

there? Like the Cathedral Square of Munster *(Figure 60)* this town hall square has a considerable number of public buildings that make up its enclosing walls. Although the curved side is explained by the former

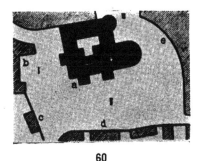

60

MUNSTER: Cathedral Square

a. Dom   b. Bischofshop   c. Museum
d. Ständehaus   e. Bank

presence of a cemetery, the Cathedral appears to be built to one side.

The magnificent grouping about the Cathedral Square of Salzburg *(Figure 61)* is pure Italian, and, as a matter of fact, it is the work of Italian masters (Scamozzi, Solari, and others). A colonnade formed by two rows of pillars (a rarity in the north) to the right and left of the Cathedral serves to separate the various plazas while preserving free passage among them. Each of the plazas forms a distinct entity, and the arrangement gives the Cathedral an advantageous relation to the Episcopal Residence. Artistic requirements and day-to-day necessities (such as easy access to the oratories) are thus equally well served.

47

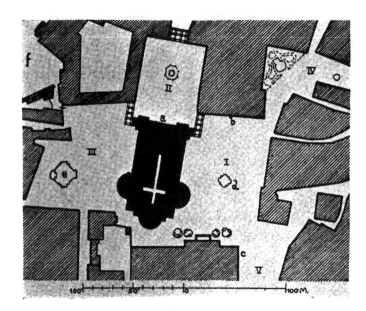

61

SALZBURG:

I. Residence Plaza
II. Cathedral Plaza
III. Capital Plaza
IV. Former Market Square
V. Mozart Plaza
a. Cathedral
b. Residence
c. Government Building
d. Fountain
e. Horse Pond
f. St. Peters

63

ROME:

The Capitol

48

The single large plaza grouping of Nuremberg *(Figure 62)*, excluding the Market Place, encloses the Egydienkirche. Its similarity to Italian plazas is not surprising since the church itself is of Italian style. But we should not attempt to distinguish between Italian plazas and those of other countries. It is more helpful to consider the

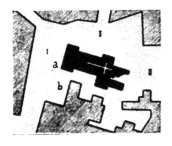

62

NUREMBERG:

Egydienplatz

a. Egydienkirche
b. Gymnasium

degree to which various plazas approach the characteristics of the ancient forum.

The oldest German building plan that consciously attempted to imitate ancient Roman style was made for the Cathedral of Hildesheim *(Figure 64)* and its surroundings. Bishop Bernard von Hildesheim, an art patron who took artists with him on his Italian travels to make sketches, appears to have been responsible for it. This took place long after the time when art teachers had been heard extolling ancient Rome. Gone was the memory of ancient splendor. Yet something of the inspiring genius of antiquity is wafted to us, even today, by the small brazen imitation of the Trajan column in the Cathedral yard at Hildesheim. The brass doors of the Cathe-dral still preserve a memory of the metal doors of the Pantheon.

Picture models of ancient Rome gradually supplanted memory of the reality. This was true even in Italy. Ancient splendor gave way to the world of medieval art, which, having attained its heights of greatness, went to its decline in a sterile imitation of the ancient forms that had preceded it. We might suppose that with the reappearance of the classical column and entablature, with the triumphant return of the gods of Olympus in poetry, painting, and sculpture, there might also be evidence of a new appearance of the Roman Forum, but that was not the case. Streets and plazas were affected by this change in style only in surface decoration. Innovations in the art of building did influence the construction of

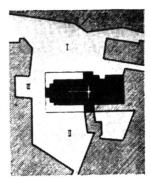

64

HILDESHEIM:

II. Greater Cathedral Yard
III. Lesser Cathedral Yard

plazas, but not according to ancient principles. Painting, sculpture, and architecture were competing in exploring the principles of perspective. A number of new architectural formulae, including a succession of new styles (Gloriette, Belvedere, etc.) sprang from this zeal for powerful effects in perspective. The creation of a new art in painting and theatrical representation was not enough. It fell to the architects to erect their buildings, monuments, fountains, and obelisks according to the same principles of perspective. Thus it was that art came to control vistas of the great three-sided plazas, churches, palaces, formal gardens, sumptuous approaches to important buildings, as well as nature's masterpieces.

A stage type of architectural setting having three enclosing sides with an open fourth side (intended as the point of view of the spectator) became the basic principle of every grouping. The full abundance of this effective principle was unquestionably an original creation of the era since it sprang from the newly matured principles of perspective. Careful searchings into history show that the beauty of the plaza in the splendid arrangement of its entirety with a masterly grouping of secondary elements often exceeded the artistic value of the buildings themselves.

This richly developed art of building cities was destined to reach its climax in Baroque styles. Like strange forebodings, some evidences of Baroque began to appear in the early Renaissance, and this requires an explanation. Each of these forerunners had a certain ingenuity which contributed to a new style. The thing that is truly astonishing is the complete oblivion into which the principles of town building

art have fallen in our own times.

Among the earliest examples of three-sided enclosed plazas, we call attention to the Plaza of the Palazzo Pitti at Florence and that of the Capitol at Rome *(Figure 63)*, begun in 1536 according to the precepts of Michelangelo. One of the finest squares of this kind, with three sides forming a coherent architectural whole, and without street intersections, is the Josephsplatz in Vienna with its unsurpassed quiet dignity. Vienna is exceptionally rich in masterly Baroque planning, and understandably so, for Vienna was a brisk center of activity for distinguished masters during the height of the period. Vienna's Piaristenplatz in its venerable confines may be regarded as an unsurpassed church plaza.

The art of Baroque architecture is even more manifest in the old castles and massive complex structures of large monasteries than it is in city planning of the period, for these groups of buildings provide us with fine examples of good building practices—placement of churches against other structures, good interior arrangement, enclosed plazas, control of perspective, and so on.

The open court enclosed on three sides became an established motif in Baroque chateaux that carried over into later construction. The numerous plans for royal residences of succeeding centuries follow this pattern almost without exception. Examples of this may be seen at Coblenz Castle *(Figure 65)*, the Würzburg

Residence *(Figure 66)*, Dresden Castle, and in many other places. Schonbrun Castle at Vienna, one of the most splendid examples of this type of layout, is appreciable from a considerable distance thanks to the effec-

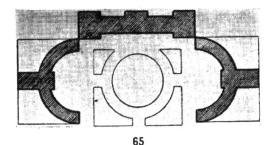

65

COBLENZ: Castle

tive approach over the stream that runs in front of the Castle.

The development of Baroque style differs from the history of earlier styles in that it did not evolve gradually. On the contrary, like modern styles, it came full panoplied from the drawing board as an invention. We cannot, therefore, attribute the banality of modern planning to the fact that it has precisely the same kind of origin. We insist, simply, that the straight line and geometrical patterns should not be made the aims of our planning.

In Baroque style there is rich ornamentation and planning to insure a pleasing appearance, not only on paper, but in reality. Control of perspective effects and skillful plaza arrangement are its outstanding features. The work of the period reached

a distinctive pinnacle in the art of city planning by means of a style which, in its essentials, must have been devised through modification of ancient principles.

The idea of a theater-type perspective, which underlies all of these groupings, is dramatically evident in castles and monumental building groups. The layout of Coblenz Castle *(Figure 65)* is also used at Dresden Castle and in many other places. Still more instructive, especially in its contrast to esteemed contemporary practices, is the ground plan of the Würzburg Residence *(Figure 66)*. Every modern university or group of public buildings laid out around large and small open spaces generally follows some variant of the Würzburg Resi-

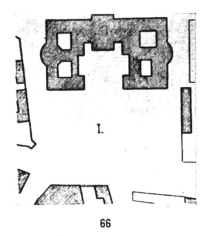

66

WÜRZBURG: Residence

dence plan—a large court or yard at the center with smaller courts at either side. This arrangement is quite popular. There are two examples of it in Vienna—the new City Hall and the University. In each it may be observed that treatment of the components of the grouping follows more recent patterns.

There is an essential difference between these modern layouts and the work of the old Baroque masters. The large court, often more expansive than an ordinary plaza, actually belongs to the interior of the building, which, seen from the outside, has the appearance of a massive block. The architect cannot be blamed for that, for the site was prescribed for him in advance according to the city plan. A different state of affairs prevailed during the Baroque period. With one side of the court left open, the enclosure with its powerful architectural effect could be advantageously seen and woven into the city structure. And which do we find the more beneficial? Again the decision is usually in favor of the old masters. We should not attribute modern shortcomings to the architects, but rather to the discredited city planning practices of our day.

The great courts adjacent to the principal buildings of Vienna are truly masterpieces of the first rank, but who sees them? It may be confidently asserted that excluding the professors and students housed in the buildings, less than five per cent of the population of Vienna have ever seen, or will see, the magnificent columned court of the University. Further study of building design will readily reveal the manner in which the architect has generally been confined to the building of his modern cubicles by rigid plotting of building sites. The fine main portal is the feature that suffers most as a result of this. Projections of this kind, with their richly sculptured enclosures and ascending approaches, by their very nature, need a certain amount of open space for effectiveness. In the absence of this, it was necessary to compress the approaches and push everything back. How much more could have been accomplished in such cases if the architect had been allowed more freedom and more control over sites and surroundings!

VIII

THERE is a surprising contrast in modern times between the art of building cities and the development of other arts, including architecture. Town building has gone its own obstinate way oblivious of everything around it. This anomaly was discernible as early as the Renaissance and in the periods that immediately followed it, but it became more dramatic later when ancient styles appeared for the second time. Classical buildings and styles were reproduced with faithful precision, and out of this enthusiasm for the art of the past, costly but impractical buildings began to spring up.

The Walhalla at Regensburg is a reflection of a Greek temple. The Loggia dei Lanzi has a modern counterpart at Munich. New churches have been built in imitation of the basilicas of the earliest Christians. Greek propylaea and Gothic domes have been put up. But what happened to the plazas that were essential to the original creations—the agora, the forum, the signoria, the market square? Nobody thought of them.

The modern city planner has become poverty-stricken as far as art is concerned. He can produce only dreary rows of houses and tiresome "blocks" to put beside the wealth of the past. We are confused and disturbed because our cities fall so short of artistic merit. In seeking sensible solutions we are bewildered when, on every occasion, "block plans" are brought out for technical discussion as though the problem were purely mechanical in its nature.

Architects, of course, can design towers, balconies, caryatids, and gables, but they are unable to get a cent for columns, porticos, arcs de triomphe or other features that could give character and art form to streets and plazas. Open space that should serve everyone actually belongs to the engineer and hygienist. All of the art forms in town building have disappeared one by one so that we have scarcely a memory of them left. Surely there is ample evidence of this.

We are perfectly aware of the great difference between our modern uniform plazas and the ancient public squares which we can still enjoy. Modern churches and monuments, we find, stand in the centers of large sites. Our streets are designed according to a chess-board pattern. They open large breaches in plaza enclosures which were formerly contained within a wall of monumental houses and buildings.

On the other hand we are charmed by the picturesque appearance of old cities. We simply overlook the methods that were used to obtain the varied artistic impressions they make.

A modern writer on city planning, R. Baumeister, in his book on urban development (page 97) says: "It is difficult to lay down a general principle concerning the factors that give a pleasing effect to a public square." Do we need more proof than this? Has not our study of ancient cities demonstrated the existence of definite principles which, set forth in great detail, could make up an entire manual and history of town building art? We would need volumes even if we confined our record to the accomplishments of the Baroque masters, who used such confident and deft skill in a wide variety of building conditions. The very fact that one of our foremost writers on the subject can make such an assertion in the face of this evidence indicates most conclusively that we have lost sight of all relationship between cause and effect.

In none of the histories of art do we find a single chapter on city building, although these books review for us, along with the work of Phidias and Michelangelo, much that has been done in bookbinding, in pewter fashioning, in costuming, and in other lesser crafts. How evident it is, then, that we have lost the continuity of artistic tradition in city building, since the very threads of continuity have become imperceptible. Let us look at the material at hand.

There is a vast body of pronouncement to explain the shortcomings of modern city planning. It continues to accumulate in the daily papers and technical journals. An occasional over-pedantic denouncement of rectangularity in the design of house elevations is about as far as this ever goes toward explaining the poor effect of our building practices. Baumeister, too, says (on page 97 of his book), "there is a just complaint against the dreariness of modern streets," and he blames the "bulky effect" of our blocks of buildings for that. With respect to the location of monuments, he tells us that "day after day new mistakes are made in the placement of monuments." But we search in vain for an explanation of the error. Compulsion to consider the center point of a plaza as the only possible location for a monument appears to be inexorable, like a natural law, as though there were some deep urgency in giving the public a rear view of the sculptured great.

Baumeister finds an illustration for one of his most discerning criticisms of modern planning in the issue of *Figaro* for August 23, 1874, which dealt with one of MacMahon's trips. "Rennes," the article said, "is not exactly unfriendly to the Marshal, but the City is incapable of civic enthusiasm. I have observed that this is true of all cities where streets are severely straight with right-angle intersections. Straight lines simply do not permit public demonstration. It could be observed in 1870 that cities of rectangular plan were easily taken, while those old towns with circuitous streets were able to defend themselves to the end."

While straight lines and right angles are the distinguishing elements of artless city plans, they do not inevitably lead to banal effects. Straight lines and right angles are also the elements of Baroque planning, which gave us effects of true artistic power. It is in street layout that rectangularity is especially hazardous. A rural road that extends for miles without a curve bores the traveler, however interesting the surrounding country may be. Its inflexible straightness, at variance with nature, cuts rigidly across the land contours. Its monotony impels us to traverse it as quickly as possible. An excessively long, straight city street has the same effect. If, however, even the shortest of streets bores us, we must seek another explanation for the defect.

Modern streets, like modern plazas, are too open. There are too many breaches made by intersecting lateral streets. This divides the line of buildings into a series of isolated blocks, and destroys the enclosed character of the street area.

A comparison of old arcades with modern imitations of them will make this clear. The old arcade, grandiose in architectural detail, runs as far as the eye can see along a street without intersection, or in an enclosure extending around a plaza, or at least without breach along one side. The whole effect depends on that, since only in that way can an arcade give the impression of being an enclosure. Modern planning produces results of a different nature. When occasionally a modern architect, inspired by this splendid old motif, attempts to reproduce it, as has been done, for example in Vienna, adjacent to the Votive Church and near the new City Hall, the resultant work scarcely resembles the original model.

The individual stalls are by far larger and more elaborately worked out than almost any of the old arcades. The desired effect, however, is not there. Why? Each separate archway is attached only to its individual block. Numerous cross streets cut the arcade into small segments so that the general effect cannot be that of an enclosure. This can be successfully overcome only by extending the portico to cover the openings of cross streets. Unless this is done, the mangled design will remain like an axe without a blade.

This explains, too, why our street arrangement does not have cohesive character. Corners usually determine the modern street plan. A string of isolated blocks of houses always presents a poor appearance, even if the street is curved.

These considerations bring us to the real nub of the matter. Modern city building completely reverses the proper relationship between built up area and open space. In former times the open spaces—streets and plazas — were designed to have an enclosed character for a definite effect. Today we normally begin by parcelling out building sites, and whatever is left over is turned into streets and plazas.

Extreme and awkward angles were formerly withdrawn from view into the building areas, but our modern plans leave the irregular wedges for plazas. We even have a cardinal principle on that point (Baumeister, page 96): "From an architectural point of view, a network of streets is a prime guarantee of suitable house sites. For that reason, right-angle street intersections are desirable."

Yes, indeed—for the architect who is afraid of an irregular site—the architect who must surely be innocent of the simplest rudiments of site planning! Without exception it is the irregular sites that present the most interesting and generally superior possibilities, for the architect is impelled by them to use ingenuity and to surpass the mere mechanical drawing of straight lines. In such a plan many secondary features like elevators, stairways, storage rooms, and lavatories can be accommodated much more readily than in symmetrical plan. It is absurd, then, to prize lots of regular shape from the architect's point of view. There is simply no basis for such a prejudice. Yet we seem to be sacrificing all beauty in design of streets and plazas to this fraudulent precept.

If we study the ground plan of a building that has been ably designed for an irregular lot, we will observe that all of its halls and rooms are well formed. The irregularities are not in view. They are hidden in the thickness of the walls, or in the secondary service features mentioned previously. Nobody wants a triangular room, for it would not only be objectionable in appearance, but it could not be pleasingly furnished. However, a circular or elliptical staircase, enclosed by walls of unequal

67

TRIESTE:

Piazza della Caserna

thickness, could easily be placed in a triangular space.

This is the way cities were planned in past ages. The forum, like a main hall, had a regular form. Its visible open space was designed to produce a desired effect. Irregularities in the plan, on the contrary, were enclosed in built-over areas or hidden in walls, a procedure both simple and clever. We follow the opposite course today, as can be shown by three examples

68

TRIESTE:

Piazza della Legna

from a single city, Trieste: the Piazza della Caserna *(Figure 67),* the Piazza della Legna *(Figure 68),* and the Piazza della Borsa *(Fig-*

ure 69). From the point of view of city building art they are not plazas at all, but simply the residue left from rectangular lot plotting. The numerous wide and poorly planned streets that open on to these three open areas make it impossible to locate monuments or worthwhile buildings in them. These triangular plazas are just as objectionable as three-sided rooms.

Let us examine this a little more closely. We have devoted an entire chapter to the irregularity of old plazas, and in it we upheld their general excellence. It might seem that this same judgment should apply

69

TRIESTE:

Piazza della Borsa

to the examples we have just described, but that is not the case, because there are two entirely different kinds of irregularity. In the case of the three plazas of Trieste, there is a discordant irregularity, emphasized by the regular lines of the surrounding buildings, which immediately strikes the eye. On the other hand, the irregularity of the old plazas that we have considered is a kind that readily gives the illusion of regularity —a kind that is more noticeable on paper than in reality. Again this is comparable to the old manner of planning buildings.

We find few precise right angles in the plans of Romanesque and Gothic churches for the old builders were unable to draw them accurately. That led to no difficulty, however, because the imperfections were not noticed. Great irregularities may also be observed in the ancient temples due to separated axes of columns, and so on; that is, they may be observed through careful measurement, but not by ordinary inspection. No importance was attached to this, however, since the sole object was a pleasing architectural effect in actuality, and not a design to be appreciated on paper.

At the same time, we can find examples of almost unbelievable ingenuity in the curvature of building frames, etc.—ingenious touches which, while scarcely measurable, were used simply because they could be readily appreciated by the eye.

The more we compare ancient methods with modern practices, the more striking is the contrast, and each succeeding comparison, from the point of view of city building art, goes against contemporary procedure. We have in mind the current groundless hesitancy to design impressively large building approaches; a suspicion of curved streets; a dreary uniformity of building heights; a striving after stark severity; endless rows of windows of similar size and design; an excess of diminutive pilasters; the perennial, miserable, little concrete scrolls, and an absence of expansive and restrained wall spaces, which are not only avoided but even replaced by false windows.

We shall, however, briefly describe the various modern systems in the next chapter and present a definite conclusion.

THE CAPITOL IN ROME

IX

Modern Systems

MODERN systems! That, indeed, is the appropriate term! We set up rigid *systems,* and then grow fearful of deviating from them by as much as a hair's breadth. Suppression, or sacrifice to system, of every ingenious touch that might give real expression to the joy of living, is truly the mark of our times.

We have three dominant systems for building cities, and a number of variations of them. They are: the rectangular system, the radial system, and the triangular system. Generally speaking, the variations are bastard offspring of these three. From an artistic point of view the whole tribe is worthless, having exhausted the last drop of art's blood from its veins. These systems accomplish nothing except a standardization of street pattern. They are purely mechanical in conception. They reduce the street system to a mere traffic utility, never serving the purposes of art. They make no appeal to the sense of perception, for we can see their features only on a map.

For that reason we have thus far avoided the term "street pattern" in discussing ancient Athens, Rome, Nuremburg, or Venice. It is really beside the point, as far as art is concerned, for artistic worth can be expected only in that which we can see, like a single street or plaza. This obvious fact will suggest that under certain circumstances almost any kind of street pattern can lend itself to artistic results, unless it has been designed with brutal heedlessness, as happened in the cities of the new world according to the dictates of the *genius loci,* and, unfortunately, as has become common in our cities.

Even the rectangular system could be used to form pleasing plazas and streets if the technician would permit the artist to look over his shoulder and change the position of his compass and T-square now and then. The two might even achieve a neat division of labor, for the artist could accomplish his purpose by designing a few of the principal streets and plazas, willingly ceding the remainder to the necessities of traffic movement and other utilitarian considerations. In work areas of the community, the city would display its working clothes, but the principal streets and plazas could be arrayed in their best for sunshine to the stimulation and pleasure of those who use them. Thus these outstanding streets and plazas could serve to foster civic pride and to fire the ambition of maturing youth.

That is exactly what we find in the old cities. Their numerous secondary streets, as a matter of fact, have little artistic significance. Only the traveler, the exceptional onlooker, finds special beauty in them, as he does in everything. Critical appraisal finds only a few principal streets and plazas in the center of the city where the old builders have achieved a rich accumulation of their clever talents in works of civic art.

This leads us to a vantage point that we must reach if, despite these modern city building systems, we are to preserve a modicum of the artistic in our cities. There is need for compromise, for if we are too exacting in what we demand for art, we will make little headway among those who are concerned with utilitarian requirements. Whoever is to succeed in upholding esthetic considerations in urban development must, first, realize that practical solutions to traffic problems are not necessarily rigid, unalterable remedies; and, secondly, he must be prepared to demonstrate that practical requirements of modern living need not necessarily obstruct artful development.

The most common modern system is the rectangular plan. It was established with inflexible permanence at Mannheim many years ago, resulting in a perfect chess board pattern for the City. Rectangularity is so completely dominant that it has even discouraged distinctive names for streets. An array of cubes extending in one direction is designated by a letter, while those files of similar cubes running in perpendicular directions are given numbers for names. Thus,

the last vestiges of old city building forms, with their undertones of imagination and fancy, have been pushed into oblivion. Mannheim boasts of having created this system. *Volenti non fiat injuria.** Whoever bothers to compile all of the condemnation and scorn inspired by the invention will be able to fill volumes with it. Surprisingly enough, however, this very system has virtually taken the whole world. No matter where we go we find that newly developed city areas have followed the rectangular plan, for even where the radial or triangular systems are in evidence, the lesser streets in the pattern are designed as closely as possible to the chess-board motif. This is especially surprising because such combinations have long been in disrepute even among those who are interested solely in the circulation of traffic. To the inconveniences in the system that these people have pointed out, we add another, which seems to have been overlooked heretofore, and that is the traffic difficulty created by intersecting streets.

Let us consider the movement of vehicles at the opening (without complete intersection) of one street into another where left turns are made *(Figure 70)*. A vehicle moving from A to C may meet another progressing from C to A, still another moving from C to B, another going from B to A, and finally another moving from B to C. There are also four possibilities for the obstruction by other vehicles of the passage of

---

*No injury is done to a consenting party.

a vehicle moving from A to B. There are but two additional possibilities for encounters between moving vehicles in the case of a vehicle moving from B to A, since all other possibilities have been accounted for in the aforementioned series. In the case of vehicles going from C to A, or from C to B, there are no possibilities for meeting other vehicles which have not already been ac-

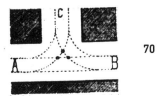

70

counted for. Without taking account of duplications, then, there are a dozen possibilities for the meeting of vehicles at this particular street junction:

AB and BA	AC and BA	BA and CA
AB and BC	AC and BC	BA and CB
AB and CA	AC and CA	BC and CA
AB and CB	AC and CB	BC and CB

Intersections of trajectories, marked by small dots on the diagram, impede traffic and can cause complete obstructions when one vehicle must wait for another to pass. However, if there are but three of these points, and if traffic is not especially heavy, there are but few cases of complete obstruction. This circumstance, the junction of a minor street with a more important thoroughfare, is commonly found in the old cities. It is, moreover, a highly practical traffic utility.

However, when the two streets completely intersect, as in Figure 71, the situation becomes much more complicated. In calculating the possible meetings of vehicles in intersections, as we did in the case of the junction of two streets, we find that there are fifty-four such possibilities, with sixteen intersections of the various trajectories, and exactly five times as many potential traffic obstructions. The path of a single vehicle going from A to B is intersected by four other paths, and a vehicle moving from C to D meets a potential obstruction in the center of the street intersection.

These intersections tend to slow traffic. Those who are accustomed to using vehicles know that it is often necessary to slow down to a walk in modern parts of cities, while much greater speed is possible in the busy, narrow streets of the old quarters. That is because the old districts rarely contain street intersections, and, as a matter of

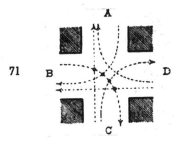

71

fact, their street junctions are relatively infrequent.

Pedestrians are imposed upon even more seriously by modern street systems.

They must leave the sidewalk for a hundred feet or so to cross a street, giving all of their attention meanwhile to the danger of vehicles approaching from the right and left. There is no continuous façade to protect them. In every city where people customarily promenade it will be observed that they instinctively choose a street with but few intersections so that the pleasure of strolling will not be incessantly disturbed by the necessity for keeping out of the way of moving vehicles.

The Ringstrasse Corso in Vienna is a perfect case in point. The inner side of the Ringstrasse is heavily used by pedestrians from the buildings of the Garden Homes Association to the elongated Kartnerstrasse, while the opposite side, which is much cooler in the summer, is usually empty. Why? Simply because a walk along the unpopular south side requires a crossing of the Schwarzenberg Plaza, a disagreeable experience. From Kartnerstrasse on to the Hofmuseen, however, the crowd suddenly switches to the opposite side of the Ringstrasse. Why? Because the pedestrian, unless he crosses at this point, must pass the rising approach to the Opera, which no longer corresponds to the natural slope of the street.

When more than four street openings converge at one point we are presented with a truly amazing traffic situation. The addition of a single junction to an intersection increases the number of potential meeting points of vehicles to one hundred and

sixty, more than a ten-fold increase as compared with the first type of junction we considered, with a consequent increase in the number of traffic obstructions. What shall we say, then, of a situation where six or more streets converge at one point *(Figure 72)?* In such a case free movement of traffic is out of the question at the busy hours of the day, and the city must place a police officer at the point to direct the movement of vehicles.

72

KASSEL:

In der Kölnerstrasze

These points of convergence are especially dangerous for pedestrians. In some places attempts have been made to overcome a few defects of this type of intersection by locating, here and there, little islands of pedestrian refuge from which rise impressive, slender lamp posts, like beacons in the midst of swelling waves of traffic. These isolated segments of sidewalk constitute, perhaps, the most important and original innovations of modern art in city building! Despite all precautionary measures, only the agile can safely cope with them. The aged and infirm avoid them by wide detours.

There you have the results of a system that has heedlessly cast aside every artistic tradition for the sole purpose of bowing to the expedients of traffic circulation. We have even called these points of traffic convergence "plazas," although they have none of the characteristics of plazas, but seem, rather, to display both the ugly

73

CASSEL:

Königsplatz

and impractical. It is the result of planning for traffic rather than planning, as should be the case, for streets and plazas.

The rectangular system produces these points of convergence wherever the

terrain is irregular or at points where new districts must be blended with the old parts of cities. This requires a departure from the chessboard pattern, or at least a modification of it, and the result is a triangular so-called "plaza." The radial system, or a combination of modern patterns, produces even more of them.

The pride of modern city planning is the circular plaza, like the Konigsplatz at Cassel *(Figure 73)*, or the octagonal plaza, like the Piazza Emanuele at Turin. There are no better examples than these of the complete absence of artistic feeling and the flouting of tradition that characterize modern city plans. Of course, these geometric plazas look quite impressive in their pretty regularity when we see them on paper,

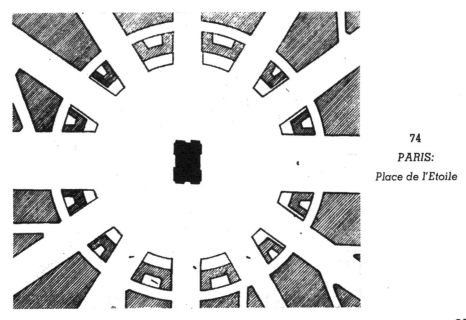

74

PARIS:

Place de l'Etoile

(Figure 74) but what is the effect in reality? They make a high virtue of parallels extending to infinity, an effect that was cleverly and artfully avoided by the old builders. They make the center of traffic movement serve also as the central point for every perspective. In walking around such a plaza the spectator retains the same view before his eyes so that he never knows exactly where he is. A single turn is enough to cause a stranger to one of the disconcerting, merry-go-round plazas to become completely lost. In the Piazza Vigliena at Palermo (Quattro Canti) the four corner buildings, although of stately architecture, are without effect for they are too much alike in design, and, while only two important streets open into this octagonal plaza at right angles, strangers frequently get lost there and wander into one of the four tributary streets in search of its name or a familiar building for reorientation. Truly we can say little for these plazas except that it is difficult to get around in them, they give us monotonous perspectives, and the buildings which enclose them cannot be set off advantageously. How odd it was of the old builders to pay such shrewd attention to these things!

This type of plaza, with its islands of pedestrian refuge and gas candelabra or columned monument, made an early appearance in Paris, although the recent regularization of the plan of that City has not made exclusive use of any modern system. That is attributable partly to the natural resistance offered by the existing develop-

ment, and partly to the tenacious manner in which the fine traditions of art seem to persevere. Hence, the procedure has been different in different parts of the City, but it might be said that a certain residue of the Baroque tradition underlies the entire work. Obviously it has carried over a deliberate working for good perspective effects. The location of monumental buildings at the termination of wide avenues has been one of its basic reforms, forming a link between modern practice and the old Ringstrasse pattern. The modern boulevard came into being when the cutting away and clearing out of tightly massed old buildings became necessary. This regularization of Paris, conceived in the grand manner, established a new style which was especially influential in the larger cities of France.

The Place Saint-Michel at Nimes *(Figure 75)* is an example of excessive opening of a plaza enclosure by the entrance of oblique streets. The Place du Pont at Lyon and other like illustrations of this might be given. This practice has something about it that harks back to the radical regularization of Rome under Nero, although it is much more cautious. New boulevards and avenues have been built at Marseille, at Nimes (Cours Neuf, Boulevard du Grand Cours, Boulevard du Petit Cours), at Lyon (Cours Napoleon), at Avignon (Cours Bonaparte), and in other cities. In Italy, wide streets of this kind, capable of accommodating several vehicles abreast with a bordering walk way, are given the name of "Corso" or

"Largo." In the north, wide rings (Ringstrasse) have often replaced the old fortified city walls. We find them in Vienna, Hamburg, Munich, Leipzig, Breslau, Hanover; at Prague between the old and new cities; at Antwerp; at Würzburg, in the form of a pentagon (Juliuspromenade, Hofpromenade, etc.); and in other places. There are many very old and isolated examples of this conception of the grand avenue, for example: Langgasse at Danzig, Breiten Gasse at Weimar, Kaiserstrasse at Freiburg, Maximilian-

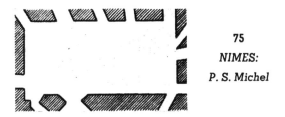

75

NIMES:

P. S. Michel

strasse at Augsburg, or Unter den Linden at Berlin. Hunters Row in Vienna is carried out entirely in the manner of this type of wide thoroughfare designed to give an impressive vista. These are forms in city building which, although modern, do have artistic merit. They are all done in the Baroque manner.

However, as soon as geometrical layouts of "blocks" became dominant, art was silenced. We find support for this assertion in the modernization that took place in Gotha, Darmstadt, Düsseldorf, the fan shaped plan of Karlsruhe, and elsewhere. The failure of these "improvements" to solve the problems of traffic movement—and that

was the sole motive for undertaking them— is proclaimed by the empty look of so many wide modern streets and plazas, in contrast to the busy activity in the old narrow streets (cf. Ludwigstrasse in Munich or the City Hall Square in Vienna). These wide thoroughfares have been built at the edges of cities, where great concentrations of traffic are not likely to occur, while the narrow streets in the heart of the city are left undisturbed.

There is evidence enough to show that those who advocate planning cities for the mere circulation of traffic, with the success they have had, are scarcely justified in casting the assistance of art, history, and the great traditions of city building to the four winds.

But let us discuss one of the really effective products of modern planning. The improved public walks and gardens are unquestionably of great hygienic value. Indisputable, also, is the charming result of bringing rustic beauty into the midst of a great city where nature's work and man's architecture can be seen in fascinating contrast. We may ask, however, whether or not proper sites have been chosen for these improvements. From a purely hygienic point of view the answer seems to be easy—the more green open space, the better. But if art is to be taken into account, we must give some thought to where and how the green open areas should be located. The most recent, and most pleasing, developments of this kind are to be seen in modern suburbs like the justly famed Suburban Village of

Frankfurt-am-Main, the Wahring Cottage Town at Vienna, similar annexations to the old city of Dresden, and in other places. However, as the rustic type of development is brought closer in to the center of the city, particularly near monumental structures, the more difficult it becomes to find an example that is generally satisfactory or artfully carried out.

Modern naturalistic landscape painting is not a suitable medium for representing grandiose subjects like mythological or religious scenes, public buildings, or churches. An attempt to harmonize it with monumental architecture would inevitably result in a disagreeable conflict in style. In exactly the same way, the location of idyllic parks in the environs of a city's principal plazas results in a clash between nature and stylistic monumentality.

The Baroque conception of the formal, trimmed park is based on a recognition of this conflict and a determination to avoid it, although our predecessors attempted landscape gardening only in connection with palaces. The magnificent plazas of antiquity, of the Middle Ages, and of the Renaissance were, above all, focal points of man's art, with emphasis on architecture and sculpture. The extent to which indiscriminate planting in them has been detrimental, especially in the shabbily planted boulevards, may be observed in photographs of outstanding buildings. Most of them are taken in winter to minimize the obstructive effect of trees and foliage. In many cases

drawings are preferable to photographs because it is possible to do away with the disturbing trees in a drawing. Does it not follow, then, that the trees are actually in the way? What is the value of a plaza, created especially to provide a view of a building, if we permit vegetation to obscure the view?

Trees should not be planted so that they can hide buildings of special interest. That is a sound principle, and it is drawn entirely from Baroque practice. It cannot be followed blindly, of course, for that would mean tearing out practically all of the planting in modern cities. Just as we have no suitable plazas for monuments, we have none for trees. In both cases the deficiency is due to the "block" system of planning.

In the older cities there is a surprising number of delightful little gardens hidden away within blocks of houses, with no exterior evidence of their presence. How different they are to the typical open arrangements of today! These old private gardens were often thrown together to form large open areas protected from wind and dust on all sides by high walls of houses. They are places of genuine relaxation for the individual owner, and they offer the entire group of householders the advantages of more light , more air, and better prospect over green open space than would otherwise be possible.

The back of a modern house usually opens on to narrow yard that is dismal, dusty, and like a miserable jail yard, often evil smelling enough to discourage the opening of windows. This keeps the tenants dissatisfied and increases the demand for houses with greater street exposure, much to the detriment of good city arrangement.

Modern parks, surrounded by open street areas, are at the mercy of wind and weather, and, unless vast dimensions give some protection, they are usually covered with dust. Thus they are without hygienic value, especially in the hot summer months when the public is most careful to avoid heat and dust.

Again the trouble is the abominable block system. The middle of a large site is quite as unsuitable for a park as it is for a building or monument. Parks need the benefit of enclosure just as buildings do. The Plaza behind the new Exchange Building at Vienna is an example of this injudicious kind of planting. As far as hygienic benefit is concerned, we may be quite sure that the trees there are of no importance whatever because they provide neither shade nor recreation. Indeed, they put forth a difficult struggle with dust and heat to withstand a withering death themselves. They succeed only in ruining the view of the Exchange. Would it not be wiser to cease the wasteful expense of this shabby kind of planting, and to build instead enclosed public parks that could offer, at least, protection from the bustle of the streets? Wherever we find an old palace garden that has been turned into a public park, we can invariably observe that it is effectively removed from vehicular movement, and that it has an en-

closed character. We will also observe that a park of this kind is of definite recreational value, and that it has flourishing vegetation.

Public desertion of miserable little park walks in favor of the sidewalks or boulevards and avenues on hot summer days is evidence of the characteristic waste and futility of this type of scattered, scrappy planting. Its chief value, perhaps, is in the evaporation of moisture on the foliage, which functions as a kind of cooling device. The slight benefits of scattered planting, however, may be sufficient to justify it, if straight rows of trees are not extended in front of monumental buildings. The artistic damage they can do under such circumstances far outweighs their almost negligible hygienic value. To interrupt planting in rows at such points is to choose the lesser of two evils.

Even in the field of gardening the discord between old and new methods prevents the use of a single kind of treatment to every part of the city. The point of departure in every layout is the historical development of the primitive unbroken street line which retains a feeling of compactness and enclosure in old cities. Modern planning follows a contrary tendency to segment everything into blocks: blocks for houses; blocks for plazas; blocks for parks; always blocks bounded by streets. This has produced the irresistible tendency to locate every kind of monument in the center of an open space.

There is a method in this madness. The block system is based on careful calculation to produce a maximum of street frontage. That, in a nutshell, accounts for the entire system. The value of a block increases with its street frontage. The greatest value is attained when the circumference of the block is as great as its area will permit. The laws of geometry, then, would indicate that circular "blocks" are of the greatest value, provided they are grouped together in the smallest possible total area, like the ranging of six circles of equal size closely around a seventh central circle. If straight streets of uniform width were then run through the connecting points, the circles would become regular hexagons, like certain types of mosaic work, or like the cells of a honeycomb. Although it is difficult to believe that anyone could be capable of doing such a banal thing, this incredible, artless type of labyrinth has actually been laid out in Chicago.* It is the purest form of the block system!

In the old world where men know the beauty and comfortable quality of venerable cities, they have not gone to that extremity. Much of the old charm has, of course, been irretrievably lost, being irreconcilable with the exigencies of modern living. But we cannot leave it all to blind chance. We must preserve as much artistic vigor as we can in our city planning. We must understand what there is that can be retained, and what there is that can be allowed to fall by the wayside. That will be the subject of the next chapter.

---

*Sitte evidently had information of a plotting plan that was never carried out. In August, 1943, a search of records in the Chicago Plan Commission was undertaken to determine the extent of this type of plotting. H. Evart Kincaid, Executive Director of the Commission, advised that the search disclosed no evidence of hexagonal plotting. The hexagonal plot, however, is seriously discussed by Robert Whitten and Thomas Adams in *Neighborhoods of Small Homes*, Cambridge, 1931. (Translator's Note.)

X

MANY of the old structural forms are simply out of the question for modern builders. While that may disturb the sentimental, it should not plunge them into a sterile nostalgia. Decorative construction without vital function is but temporary and of questionable value. Time makes inexorable changes in community life, and these changes alter the original significance of architectural forms.

Important events of today are published in the newspapers, rather than by public criers, as was done in ancient Greece and Rome, and we cannot change that. Retail trade has made a steady progression from the market square into dull buildings and the pedler's satchel, and we cannot change that. Fountains have been reduced to mere decorative function by the piping of water directly into houses, and that is not a thing we would change. Popular festivals, parades, religious processions, and open-air theatrical events will soon be but memories.

As the slow succession of the centuries has removed feature after feature of civic activity from public open places, it has shorn the plaza of its principal purpose. Artistic city development got more encouragement from the quality of ancient life than it does from our severely regulated modern existence, for modern ideas of urban beauty differ from the old in basic character as well as in detail.

Great population increases in our modern capitals, more than anything else, have shattered the old forms. With the growth of a city its streets widen and its buildings grow taller and bulkier. With their colossal dimensions, numerous stories, and endless rows of monotonous windows, they can scarcely make a pleasing impression. Appreciation of style has, at length, become so blunted by the incessant dreariness of modern architecture, that only an exceptionally striking effect can now arouse interest. But we cannot turn the clock back, and consequently the modern planner, like the modern architect, must draw his plans for a metropolis to the scale of several million inhabitants.

Intense human concentration has meant intense increase in land value, and neither the individual nor city government can escape the consequences. Subdivision and street opening have proceeded apace. Street after street has been cut through old districts, giving birth to more and more city blocks. This has been an inevitable result of high land value and greater demand for street frontage. Simple rules of art can hardly be expected to solve all the problems that confront us. We must accept these things as the given conditions of an art problem, just as physics and statics are taken into account by the architect even though they put restrictions on the freedom of his work.

It is difficult to overcome the economic effects of rectangular lot plotting, but we cannot submit blindly to the practice. To do so is to fan the flames that threaten civic beauty. Gradual demolition for the sake of rectangularity is already making inroads upon some of the charmingly varied old streets of Nuremberg, Heilbronn, and Gorlitz.

High land costs encourage greater intensity of land use, and this, in turn, suppresses certain structural forms. Modern lot plotting tends to exalt the cube motif in architecture. Ledges, court yards, arcades, free standing towers, and magnificent outdoor stairways have become prohibitive luxuries for us. Even in the design of public buildings the architect must curb his ingenuity in designing balconies, bay windows, or projections of any kind. The tendency to stick to the "building line" is so deeply entrenched in modern practice that it has virtually outmoded worthwhile structural forms like the outdoor stairway. We still have them as interior features. They have fled from the open places as though to take refuge from the invasion of traffic.

How can we compensate for the interesting features that have thus become atrophied? How would the municipal buildings of Leiden or Bolswaert look if we removed their imposing exterior staircases? What kind of impression would the Heilbronn City Hall make if we took away its two monuments and its outer stairs? These minor structures, although impractical under the limitations imposed by modern conditions, enhance the beauty and splendor of a whole city. Notwithstanding this, no contemporary architect would dare suggest anything like the charming grouping of a magnificent staircase, terrace, rostrum, and statue that we find near the City Hall of Gorlitz. The remarkable stairways, arcades, and balconies appurtenant to the old city buildings of Lübeck and Lemgo are among the delightful riches of the past. They are marked by the spirit of their times. We marvel at the Palace of the Doges at Venice and the Capitol at Rome, but nobody suggests that we build such structures now. We admire the great staircases that ornate the town halls of Halberstadt, Brussels, Deventer, Hoogstraeten, La Haye, and Rothenburg, but modern practice is hostile to the grand stairway. The mere thought of snow and ice is enough to banish all visions of the past. More than that, the grand stairway has become an interior feature in this age of indoor living. We have become such inveterate indoor creatures, having brought public gatherings inside from the plazas and streets, that we can scarcely work or dine with open windows.

Outdoor use of certain interior features like stairs and halls was an essential charm of ancient and medieval city building. The picturesque character of Amalfi, for example, is derived from an amazing mixture of various indoor and outdoor features. The effect is such that one feels that he is both inside a building and out in the open space at the same time, and that he is on the ground level and on one of the upper stories at the same time. That is because it is difficult to encompass the varied combinations at once. Places like this were the original stage settings that the theater later sought to imitate in backdrops. It is most unlikely that our dull modern layouts will ever serve as models for dramatic settings.

In this modern conflict between the fanciful and the practical, the picturesque is put aside and emphasis is placed on crass utility. Although we would not be likely to substitute sheer work-a-day practicality for beauty in the theater, we have done it in our cities with rectangular blocks. Of course it would be desirable to have an abundance of effective motifs, and if somehow we should have an increase in interesting street irregularities, broken or circuitous street lines, streets with non-parallel sides, varied building heights, outer stairways, balconies, bay windows, gables and all the things that make up the picturesque furniture of dramatic architecture, no modern city would suffer by it. However those who have more than a literary acquaintance with the problem—those who have actually engaged in building—know perfectly well that many barriers stand in the way, so many in fact that at first glance nothing at all seems possible.

Complete translation of ideal conception into actuality is impossible for a large grouping of picturesque details whose charm depends upon the incomplete and ancient. Decay and even dirt with its varied colors and textures can be made attractive in pictures, but it is not so in reality. An old castle may be very fine for a short summer visit, but a new building with its numerous conveniences is preferable for permanent residence. We should be blind indeed to overlook the tremendous benefits in sanitation that modern city building has given us. In this the engineers that we have criticized so roundly have done wonders in rendering an everlasting service to humanity. Their work has wrought remarkable improvement in the public health of European cities as can be shown by declining death rates, which in many cases have been reduced by one-half. That result reflects untold improvement in the general welfare of every city dweller. Paying enthusiastic tribute to this basic public benefit, it may still be asked whether the price for it need be stripping beauty from our cities.

Conflict between the utilitarian and the beautiful cannot be resolved. It will go on because of its very nature. That kind of struggle between two opposing forces is not peculiar to the art of building cities. It is inherent in all of the arts, even those that appear to have the greatest freedom. There is always a conflict between the artistic objective and the restrictions imposed by the artistic medium. A completely unhampered work of art may be possible in the abstract, but never in perceptible reality. The practical artist can carry out his ideas only within the limits imposed by technical feasibility. Those who familiarize themselves with the history of the arts will understand that these limitations are more or less severe depending upon the nature of technical expediency and the practical demands of a given era.

At present there are severe limitations upon art in building cities. We can no longer create a superior, finished work of art like the Acropolis of Athens. Even if the tremendous cost were supportable, we lack the basic art idea—a universally accepted explanation of reality throbbing in the daily life of the people—that could find expression in such a work. Even as superficial decoration without vital significance, it would still be beyond the reach of nineteenth century materialism. The contemporary city builder must, above all, proceed with modest circumspection, not so much because of a lack of money as because of a lack of a genuine, vital, fundamental approach.

If we should now undertake a new development to be both grandiose and picturesque, designed to express and exalt civic life, we should need, in addition to accurate design, the colors of the old masters, to obtain results like theirs. We should have to create curves, recesses, and irregularities by artificial means, or, in other words, to force spontaneity. Is it really possible to plan on paper the kind of effect that was produced by the passage of centuries? Could we actually derive any satisfaction from feigned naïveté and sheer artificiality? Certainly not. These charming effects must be foresworn in an age that no longer builds little by little as circumstances at the site suggest, but instead carries on its construction according to calculations made at the drawing board. We cannot go back through the centuries, and consequently we cannot expect to reproduce much of the picturesque quality that we associate with the old cities. Modern life and modern building methods prevent a servile imitation of old city arrangement. We must never lose sight of that fact, lest we become hopelessly sentimental. The vitality of the glorious old models should inspire us to something other than fruitless imitation. If we seek out the essential quality of this heritage and adapt it to modern conditions we shall be able to plant the seeds of new vitality in seemingly barren soil.

This attempt should not be deterred, no matter how great the discouragements may be. We can make full allowance for the requirements of modern building practices, public health, and traffic circulation without abandoning every artistic consideration. These things need not force us to reduce city building to a mere technical procedure like the building of a road or a machine, for even in our busy day-to-day activity we cannot forego those noble impressions that engender artistic conception. It must be remembered that art has a legitimate and vital place in civic arrangement, for it is this kind of art alone that daily and hourly influences the great mass of the people, while the influence of the theater and concert hall is generally confined to a relatively small segment of the population. Public planning authorities should take this factor into careful consideration and, as far as is possible, harmonize the essential old principles with present day necessities. We shall elaborate on that subject in the following final chapters.

XI

Improved Modern Systems

OUR study has already indicated the obvious need for innovations to overcome the effects of the ill-famed rectangular system. Analysis of old plans has hinted at some improvements. First of all, however, it is worth while to present a number of examples, drawn from modern innovations, to show that beauty

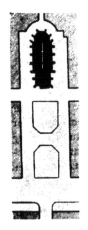

76

WIESBADEN:

*Die katholische Kirche
am Luisenplatz*

and coherence are still attainable in spite of restraints and artistic limitations imposed by practical expediency.

All of the after-influences of the Baroque tradition belong in this category. In them we find many effective and deliberate uses of worthy principles, although

they merit but occasional general approval here and there in ground plans of horseshoe shape or in the treatment of the foreground of monumental buildings. Superior layouts, if weak and confused, have resulted from mixing various styles. Thus, while the placement of the Catholic Church on Louise Plaza at Wiesbaden *(Figure 76)* is much better than the commonly selected center of a regular open place, it is spoiled

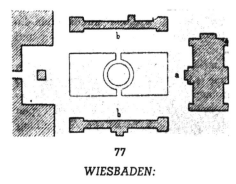

77

WIESBADEN:

a. Kursaal   b. Kolomaden

by the inevitable block system. Similarly, the horseshoe pattern formed by the Kursaal Building *(Figure 77)* and the two colonnades at Wiesbaden is quite good. However, the absence of any kind of connection between structures for the sake of enclosed character, and the consequent isolation of

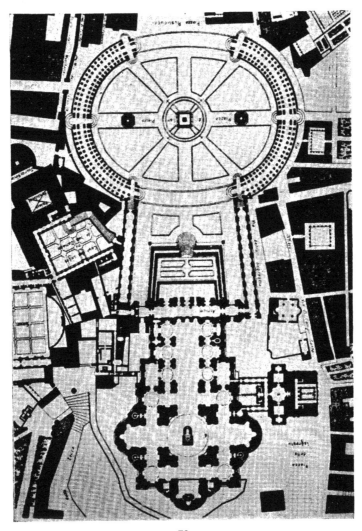

78

ROME: St. Peters and The Plaza

the various structures, is beyond explanation when we recall the vigorous Baroque style, but there is here a sufficiently clear indication that cohesive and significant effects are still attainable.

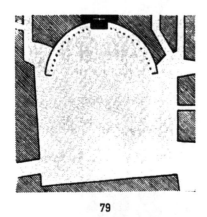

79

NAPLES: Piazza del Plebiscito

In modern expansion and regularization of cities the recent work at Paris has deviated the least from the great Baroque tradition. Paris, having within it all of the difficulties of a vast metropolis, has shown in this that deliberately sought perspective effects are possible even within the limitations imposed by practical considerations.

There were ancient forerunners of modern plans, especially in Rome, which, due to its character and importance as a great city, had to develop in the modern manner to some extent to accommodate enormous crowds. These plans merit careful study, for although they stem from a period rich in artistic creation, they also had

to be adjusted to practical urban requirements not unlike those of the present. The most significant arrangement of this kind is the well known Plaza of St. Peter's at Rome *(Figure 78)*. Its principal feature, the elliptical enclosure, is typically Roman, for it is not only frequently used in Rome, but undoubtedly it is derived from the form of the ancient Roman arena and amphitheater. It persists partly through imitation and partly through its indigenous character, as is the case in the Piazza Navona. Remember, too, the circular form of the colossal Piazza del Popolo. From Rome this plaza style spread throughout Italy and beyond its boundaries. The Piazza del Plebiscito at Naples *(Figure 79)* and the partially rounded plaza before the Church of St. Nicholas at Catania *(Figure 80)* give evidence of this.

80

CATANIA:

S. Nicolo

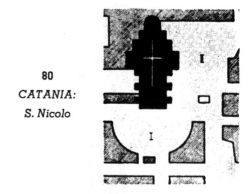

The Bastille (Zwinger) at Dresden *(Figure 81)* is one of the most interesting examples of this kind in the north. This ostentatious structure was left incomplete. One side remained open, and the area between this open side and the nearby bank of the Elbe River was for a long time covered with a neglected foundry works. It so happened that on one occasion when no suitable site could be found in all Dresden for an equestrian statue, Gottfried Semper was asked for an opinion on the problem. Semper's reply was in the form of a new city plan, one of the most interesting of its kind produced in recent years. It outlined for Dresden the finest arrangement conceived since the building of St. Peter's.

His plan called for razing the foundry works in front of the Bastille to permit the creation of a forum type of plaza in its place between the monumental buildings. Semper proposed that all of the major public buildings then contemplated be joined here to create a magnificent center of interest. The principal axis of the entire grouping was to extend from the Bastille to the Elbe. A new theater was to stand opposite the Court Church. The regal greenhouse and the museum were planned to balance the theater and to connect it with the Bastille. A magnificent landing place, reached by imposing stairs and bedecked with monumental standards like those of St. Mark's, was to be built at the edge of the Elbe, and the entirety of the splendid plaza was ultimately to be embellished with monuments.

Had all that been faithfully carried out, this plaza would have been overpowering in its effect. Indeed, it would have attained lasting fame as a work of supreme

worth. However, the convincingly lucid conception was stubbornly resisted by the dull, petty spirit of the time until it became

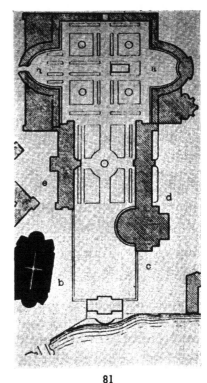

81

DRESDEN:

Plaza of the Zwinger as Planned

by G. Semper

a. Zwinger   c. Court Theater
b. Court Church   d. Greenhouse
e. Museum

vitiated and ruined. First the greenhouse was put on an insignificant street corner. Then the theater was built on the planned site, and finally the museum was used as a fourth side of the Plaza to shut in the Bastille.

The Bastille and the museum are without relation to each other in this planless and pointless arrangement. The theater stands isolated in the desolate emptiness of the plaza. Orientation and effectiveness are absent. The opportunity for achieving a cohesive and harmonious grouping in this confusion of haphazardly located buildings, that stand in disarrangement like the merchandise in a furniture store, has been cast aside forever. Not only does the City of Dresden suffer because of this, but there is a genuine loss to all who appreciate fine art—to all those visitors who could have derived intense pleasure from the magnificent plaza and who might have been able to take away with them a memory of lasting satisfaction.

Gottfried Semper had another opportunity to propose the same conception on an even grander scale in the building plan for the new Palace buildings and Court museum at Vienna *(Figure 82)*. This plan, essentially the same as that proposed for Dresden, is derived in style from St. Peter's at Rome, and, through that, from the ancient Roman design. The plaza will be an imperial forum in the truest sense of the term. Its prodigous dimensions, 788 feet long and 427 feet wide, almost equal those of St. Peter's. The fates have been kinder in this case than they were to the Dresden plan. Work is progressing to its completion.

This indicates that in spite of discouragements in the trend of the times, true splendor and beauty are possible when a competent artist finds proper support against fashionable bad taste.

We have had some recent success even in locating monuments in the grand manner, although, unfortunately, this has been an exception to the general practice. Vienna, particularly, has had more success than failure with its recently erected large monuments; that is, with respect to site selection, which is our sole consideration here. The excellently oriented Schubert

83

VIENNA:

a. Haydn-Monument vor der Kirche zu Mariahilf

Monument has a snug, appropriate place in the foliage of a city park, and the Haydn Monument *(Figure 83)* has a site well adapted to its dimensions.

The lofty *columna rostrata* of the Tegetthoff Monument is admirably suitable at the end of a boulevard type of thoroughfare like Praterstrasse. It is unfortunate that the round plaza of the Pratersterne (which could have only a slender column or obelisk as an appropriate form in its center) has not been given an architectural treatment ap-

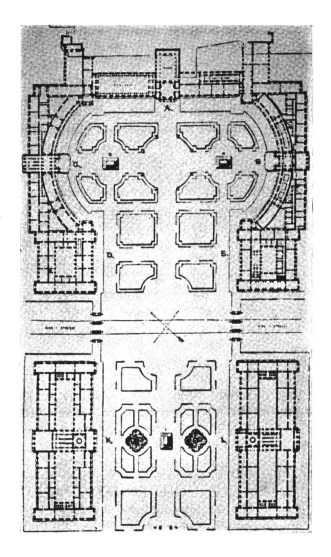

82

VIENNA:

A, B, C, D, E, New Palace Building; G, Monument of Archduke Charles; H, Monument of Prince Eugene; I, Monument of the Empress Maria-Theresa; K, Museum of Natural History; L, Museum of Art History.

propriate to the Monument. A vigorous columnar architectural treatment of two interlaced masses, carried around the entire semicircle, is the only possible remedy for this. Would it not be possible to locate a future central railroad station or some similar structure here for that purpose?

As this goes to the printer a site for the Radetzky Monument has finally been selected in the courtyard of the War Ministry Building, and hence at the edge of the Plaza. Its orientation submits to two alternatives. It may be located with respect to the principal axis of the Plaza, or with respect to the principal axis of the War Ministry Building. In the first case the monument would necessarily stand in the axis of the Plaza and its consequent relationship to the Plaza as a whole is obvious. In the second case, however, it would necessarily be moved out of the axis of the Plaza toward the War Ministry Building. The effect of this is also apparent at once, even to the uninitiated; that is, we should have the proper result of building and monument standing in significant relationship to each other. Thus, either location would be good.

The proportions and location of the Empress Maria Theresa Monument may be cited as evidence of masterly execution. The powerful architecture of the Court Museum, the immense size of the Plaza, and the bold placement of the Monument required a finished and versatile skill. The grouping enhances each of the component parts. Even the contour of the Monument is

in harmony with the dominating domes of the two museums. The relationship between these and the four smaller corner domes gives further repetition to the movement of the Monument's contour line—an example of pure three-part harmony.

Thus we have a few examples of successful monument placement in recent years in those isolated cases where the abilities of the artist have, at least, prevented gross errors. In general, however, this particular art has suffered through the scattering of monuments through all the plazas and street corners of a city. We find a fountain here and a statue there. Only in the rarest cases do we find a successful, attractive grouping of monumental buildings and monuments.

Even the smallest city can have the pleasant advantage of a superb and distinctive plaza if it locates all of its important buildings and monuments there in a well arranged assembly, as at an exposition, so that each complements the effect of the others. The purpose of a city plan is to make such an idea intelligible and attainable. No artistic objective, however, is more stubbornly resisted by the modern block system than this. If the lots are plotted according to the unfortunate rectangular system and officially approved for sale, then it is useless to attempt distinctive development in the part of the city so planned.

That is why we find tolerable success in modern lot plotting only when, due to demolition of old buildings or removal of old fortifications, it has had to be adapted to the plan of an old city; while nearly all entirely new development, especially that undertaken on level ground, results in failure. This suggests the problem of preserving some artistic vision in this unrestricted rectangular plotting of lots.

The readily conceded and conspicuous failure of city expansion during the past decade is clear indication that some foresight must be used to this end. It is generally recognized that rectangular plotting is incompatible with artful results, and there is a disposition to allow more freedom in the use of traditional principles in new development. Out of this recognition, as early as 1874, the general conference of the German Association of Architects and Engineers, meeting in Berlin, adopted the following resolution (see "Deutsche Bauzeitung 1874"):

"1. Planning for urban expansion is essentially the establishment of principal features of the various means of communication: streets, tramways, steamways, and canals, with provision for systematic and considerable extension.

"2. The street plan should, at first, comprise only the principal arteries, with careful regard to existing roads wherever feasible, and lesser streets as determined by local conditions. Plotting of lots may be undertaken in accordance with needs of the immediate future, or left to private activity.

"3. The grouping of different city areas should be done through appropriate site selection and by considering characteristic features; compulsorily, only through public health laws applicable to industry."

This was a conclusive leave-taking from every kind of plotting system, and thus it was decidedly a step in the right direction, although there is no tangible evidence that it has been heeded. An annoying prosaic quality hangs like a curse over plotting procedure just as it did before the resolution was adopted. This is quite understandable, for the three points are almost wholly negative or restrictive, which is a general characteristic of modern art criticism and esthetics. They contain but a single positive injunction—take "careful regard to existing roads wherever feasible."

This disposition to oversimplify city planning was, essentially, no more than a vote of "no confidence" in those who were then charged with the responsibility of planning. Adoption of the resolution was primarily intended to withdraw as much of this work as possible from notoriously inept hands. In this light, the action is truly significant in that it suggests the impossibility of achieving a good city plan through official action alone. To expect this would be just as unreasonable as to expect the building of cathedrals, the painting of great pictures, or the composition of symphonies through public action. A work of art can be created only by an individual. An artfully effective city plan is truly a work of art, and not a matter of administrative routine. That is the essence of the entire problem.

Even if we assume that every official has the ability, knowledge, background in travel and training, innate artistic feeling, and imagination to conceive of an effective city plan, a number of officials acting together in a bureau would produce only barren, pedantic stuff of a dusty official flavor. The department executive has no time to do the work himself, burdened as he is with conferences, reports, commissions, administration, and so on. The subordinate official dares not intrude his own ideas. He must abide by the official standard. His drawing board has no other inspiration, not that he isn't capable of something better, but because his work is official. Personal ambition, artistic individuality, and enthusiasm for work of one's own responsibility are factors that do not fit into public administration. In fact, they are incompatible with official discipline.

Thus the resolution might have been reduced to the mere statement that official monopoly in city planning, unassisted by any kind of artistic force, had established an unfortunate precedent. It might also have indicated a course of future action and the principles to be followed. But there are no such guiding formulae, everything being left to the favor of circumstance. This was also true in ancient times, but the results then were magnificent.

It would be a grievous error to assume, however, that unguided circum-stance could today result in artful expression, as it did in past historical eras. Although splendid plazas and city plans came into being without plot plans, without collaboration, and without other evident painstaking measures, they were not produced by mere chance or caprice. They developed gradually in a process that was not accidental. Individual builders, far from acting upon mere whim, unwittingly and in concert, followed the artistic tradition of the age, and they followed it with a confidence that invariably produced superior results.

When the Roman established his camp he knew exactly what to do. It never occurred to him to depart from established practices, for they satisfied his requirements with respect to convenience and beauty. When the camp later developed into a city, it was, of course, necessary for it to have a forum with its grouping of temples, public buildings, and statues. Everyone understood these practices and conformed to every detail, for there was but one traditional pattern that varied only with local conditions. Thus it was not chance, but a great artistic tradition living in the people that determined the character of city building. Even without plans the ancients avoided aimlessness, as did the builders of the Middle Ages and the Renaissance.

Where would the same kind of dependence upon circumstance lead us today? Without a city plan and without standards every builder would follow a different course, for there is no longer a definite artistic tradition living within the great mass of the people, and the result would be an awkward, confused hodge-podge. We would have the most artless kind of development. Isolated blocks of houses would spring up. Buildings would be located here and there without relation to other struc-

84

*Typical location
of a Church*

(After Baumeister)

tures. Precise geometric regularity would be the basis for plotting lots. Churches and monuments would be placed in the centers of their sites, for that is perhaps the single element of urban beauty that seems to be taken for granted today.

R. Baumeister's work on plans for

85

city expansion provides convincing proof of this view. While Baumeister fully supports the conclusions of the Berlin conference, and while he hurls devastating criticism at common modern practices in city building, his own city plans do not vary one iota from the worst of them. The proper location for a church, in his plans, is in the middle of a plaza *(Figure 84)*. Other features of his plans

simply illustrate modern mistakes without giving us a single reflection of traditional art *(See Figures 85-88)*. All of them introduce awkward street arrangements with all of the consequent evils: clogged circulation; the impossibility of well set-off buildings; improper location of monuments; and the

86

absence of a unified artistic character in the plaza as a whole. His only original proposals are "more frequent intersection of streets through plazas and complete freedom for the setting back of building lines." We shall not bother to discuss these scanty counsels. It is most unfortunate that such practices have become typical, for they repudiate every lesson of the past and obstruct the needs of art.

87   88

We cannot banish the difficulty by leaving the molding of city building to circumstance. At all costs we must formulate art's claims in a positive manner for we can no longer rely on general feeling in matters of art. We must study the works of the past and replace our loss in artistic tradition by seeking out the elements of beauty in ancient works. These elements of effectiveness must become essential principles of modern city building. Only in that way can we expect to progress, if indeed it is at all possible. After the analysis of essentials, which has formed the first part of our study, a formulation of principles will be possible in the final conclusions.

Obviously a planner cannot plan a new city area in an artful manner without a definite idea of what it is to be, what public buildings will be in it, and what plazas it is to have. He cannot begin work until he has taken probabilities of use into full account. Only in that way can his plan conform to the topography, fulfill the essential requirements, and permit an artistic development of the area. To proceed in any other way would be like expecting an architect to begin work after being told to "build something to cost about one hundred thousand dollars." Residential investment property, the architect might ask. "No." A villa? "No." A factory perhaps. "No." And so on. That kind of procedure would be ridiculous, even insane, and it doesn't happen because nobody builds a building without some purpose in mind, and consequently nobody commissions an architect without having a building program.

Only in city building, apparently, is it considered sane to prepare a building plan without a definite building program. In this field it is quite usual to go ahead with the plan but without any idea as to how the new district is to be developed. The city block with its monotonous lot plotting is the striking expression of this uncertainty. Planning attempts of this kind simply say, in their barren way, "We could certainly do something useful and beautiful, but we don't know what, and so we humbly lay aside the problem which was never stated in sufficient detail to suit us, and neatly divide the surface into regular parcels so that sales by the square foot may begin."

What a departure this is from the ideal of the ancients! And we have not been indulging in caricature. This little scene is a true portrayal of the facts. A block system of this kind has been ruled for a new district in Vienna and stands now as the plan for the so called new Danube City. It is as poor and as awkward a plan as could be devised.

The division of North America into states was a gigantic block plan that illustrates the unfortunate results of planning without a program. This vast country was divided by straight lines according to degrees of latitude and longitude, and its consequent imperfections are striking. At the time it was done the country was unknown. Having no past, and representing but so many square miles of land to civilization, America's future development could not be foreseen. This same rectangular system of dividing land, when applied to cities, was perhaps satisfactory for the cities of America, Australia, and other new countries. The inhabitants of those cities were primarily concerned with survival. They lived only for gainful production, and produced only to live. It mattered little to them that they were packed up in barracks like herring in casks.

Good planning depends upon the existence of an actual program. The necessary preliminary studies can be made by official agencies or by expert commissions. They should include:

A. An estimation of population growth in the planned area projected fifty years into the future; a study of the needed type of circulation and buildings, including the desirable location for dwellings, large homes, commercial buildings, and factories, for the purpose of either grouping similar types of structures or for planning mixed uses.

The objection that such estimates cannot be made with even approximate accuracy is but a poor excuse to escape a responsibility which, admittedly, is a difficult one. Whoever goes into the history of a city, carefully studies its commercial and industrial development along with related statistical material, and probes into local characteristics, will be sufficiently equipped with points of reference to project a great many factors into the immediate future with reasonable safety, and there is no need for more than this. Clearly, if there is not courage enough to project something of a definite nature, then the kind of dwellings built expressly for let will spring up everywhere, for this dreary and monotonous type of structure can be put up on any kind of site.

The absorption of cities by blocks of rent houses should be checked lest it become complete as an expression of uncertainty and indecision. This has already been done at Villenviertel (Wahring Cottage Town at Vienna, etc.), and it is essential to any plan for development of character and individuality.

The worst type of rent dwelling section may be observed in embryo in the gradual development of Danube City now getting under way. It certainly should not be necessary to allow this premature spoiling of such a prominent place which might well become a showplace of the future in Vienna. Consider Budapest where stand the finest and most greatly admired urban areas along the Danube, where the river is made a magnificent feature of the City itself. Sooner or later the Danube can have an equally fine effect on Vienna. It may be slow in coming, but come it must because all of the geographical requirements for it are present. Should, then, a gradual slum development be permitted in the meantime? Should not the senseless and immensely costly rectangular system be abandoned? Who is there that would undertake to defend it today? Or does anyone think that further development of Vienna should be renounced for all time? The indiscriminate building of barracks on the magnificent sites along the Danube should be stopped without delay. Otherwise, the potential vistas and mountain panoramas of its banks will be permanently spoiled by dismal hovels.

Perhaps this example might be interpreted as an indication that planning is possible without a program. To our statement that planning requires a program, should be added the proviso that unless a program is formulated, actual development will follow the poorest of all possible alternatives.

B. On the basis of these essential studies a calculation should be made of the probable number, size, and form of public buildings needed in the planned area. This can be greatly facilitated by statistical material that is readily available in most cases. An estimate of population growth will determine the number and size of churches, schools, public buildings, market buildings, public gardens, and perhaps even of a theater.

After this is done the actual planning can begin in determining the best location and grouping of the various buildings. Public competitions should be held for this. In addition to the data already described, certain other information should be assembled for use in such public competitions. It should include a relief map showing existing roads and features of special interest in the area, data pertaining to prevailing winds, water levels, and other factors of particular local importance.

Contestants should strive for the most suitable and artful location and grouping of necessary public buildings, parks, and so on. For example, a number of parks might be spaced at equal distances from each other, and arranged so that each would be enclosed by houses rather than left completely open (for reasons that have been discussed). Access to the interior of each park could be provided by two or more appropriate portals of varied design. An arrangement like this can afford the greatest possible protection to park areas and establish worthwhile sites. At the same time it can provide a first-rate defense against encroachment of the block system.

If, on the contrary, it is desired to spread parks widely apart, then it is necessary to group public buildings like churches, parsonages, schools, etc. about them in a suitable manner. In any event it is desirable to group monuments, fountains, and public buildings so that, at least, they can permit a plaza of effective expanse, and if there are to be a number of plazas it is likewise better to have groupings of these plazas than to scatter them widely apart. Each plaza should have its individual character and interest as determined by its location, size, and shape, as well as a suitable arrangement of street openings and a closed-in form. Consideration should be given to good perspectives of natural features. The propitious horse-shoe form of plaza favored in Baroque planning, entrance courts like the ancient atrium, and other like forms of known effectiveness should be kept in mind for use in opportune circumstances. Churches and monumental buildings should not, of course, be left free standing. Rather, they should form part of the plaza enclosure so that good locations for future monuments and fountains will be provided around the edges of the plaza.

Rugged terrain, water courses, and existing roads should not be ruthlessly obliterated for the sake of a stupid rectangularity. On the contrary, they should present welcome occasions for deviating street lines and other informalities. Irregularities of this kind, so often removed at tremendous expense in these days, are absolute necessities. Without them a certain rigidity and cold affectation descends upon even the finest works. Moreover, it is precisely these irregularities that provide easy orientation in the street network.

They have value, too, from the standpoint of public health. Circuitous and crooked streets in old cities break the wind so that even at high velocity it sweeps only over rooftops. In contrast to this, high winds blow through the regularized streets of modern cities to the point of discomfort and unhealthiness. It is easy to become convinced of this in any place where modern city development stands adjacent to an old district. Perhaps the best example is in wind-blessed Vienna. While it is possible for a pedestrian to stroll without discomfort in the old inner city, he is immediately enveloped in clouds of dust when he steps into a modern part of the City. Open plazas, where street openings draw in wind from every direction (like the new City Hall Plaza of Vienna) feature beautiful wind spirals throughout the year—dust columns in summer and snow flurries in winter. This is one of the pretty spectacles made possible by modern advances in city building!

Buildings like Gothic cathedrals that rise high above surrounding roof tops have a special effect on air currents in that they break the wind and send it burrowing into the hollows. For that reason the narrow circumferential passages around cathedrals are rarely free of wind. An amusing old doggerel says this of the Cathedral of St. Stephan in Vienna:

St. Stephan's does in Vienna bide.
It's grey without and dark inside.
Oh have you seen the front view here?
Then walk around and see the rear.
There you will have another view
If blowing wind allows you to.

Perhaps it would be well to locate such a church so that the choir is against the prevailing wind. Thus the silhouette of the choir and the high towers would form, in their entirety, an oblique surface to deflect brisk wind currents to higher levels rather than toward the ground; and the roof of the nave, like an inverted ship's keel, would divide the winds. Vitruvius pointed out that the orientation of streets should be determined as much by the direction of prevailing winds as by the points of the compass. Our highly scientific modern city building has forgotten all about that, and has developed a facility for making every possible mistake.

These various preliminaries would result in a number of planned building sites, provision for a large park arrangement with an unbroken enclosure of houses, and plans for a number of plazas of a certain size and form. After that, attention should be given to the establishment of the principal ways of communication and to other local considerations. This brings us to the starting point for carrying out the plan within the terms of the resolution of the Berlin Conference of the Engineers and Architects Association.

Nevertheless the task is scarcely half done, for the features of the plan, as completed up to this point, tend to succumb to the rectangular block system. Great care is needed to see that a properly initiated work is preserved from degeneration. The supervision of good taste and a continued application of artistic ability should be provided for by means of repeated competitions, or by other means, during the course of development.

It would be profitable to combine the competition for a plaza, or for a larger development, with competitions for the various public buildings that are to be located around the plaza. Perhaps that is the best way to insure perfect harmony between buildings and plazas, for it would require the design of the entirety as a unified conception. Freed from the customary restrictions of a minutely defined parcel of land, the competing architects could achieve a variety and vigor in their buildings far superior to the ungainliness which the block system enforces upon our finest structures. The Baroque masters were able to derive

an abundance of variety in motif from simple regularity, but complete domination of rectangularity in plotting has since compressed every structural form into a single motif, and the least interesting of them all, the cube.

There must be freedom in the design of a plaza to bring life and movement into the architectural ensemble, and there must be sustained watchfulness over details to prevent a well conceived arrangement from coming to a bad end. City planning is truly a vast and arduous undertaking.

The history of a venerable old city is like a ledger to account for the tremendous sums of spiritual, mental, and artistic capital that have been invested in it. Capital of that kind pays perpetual dividends by its glorious effect on mankind. Close study will indicate that the value of this dividend, like a material dividend, is in proportion to the amount of invested capital, and that realization of dividend depends upon wise investment of capital.

There is disgracefully little investment of this kind of capital in a modern block layout. Block sizes and street widths are generally fixed by some kind of ordinance or resolution. After that, plans for new developments can be made by the lowliest copyist in the bureau, or by its janitor, if we are not too particular about neatness. Such planning is without artistic value, and, as may be observed in tiresome modern cities, it produces no worthwhile effects. It contributes nothing to the satisfaction of the urban citizen, gives him no cause for pride in his city or reason for loyalty to it. This consideration should enable our calculating, materialistic age to see the value of an artful city arrangement.

A great deal has been written about the importance of fine arts to the national economy. It will be generally agreed that the pure ideal significance of art is its own end, perhaps even the highest end of human activity and civilized effort, but there are social and economic values inherent in art—the stimulation of local patriotism and fondness for home; attraction of foreign travelers and increased business with them. Surely in view of this the coldest official economist can be induced to sanction expenditures for good taste in city planning.

Whatever approach is made to the problem of city planning inescapably leads to the conclusion that the subject has been too lightly dealt with in recent times. It needs much more intelligent handling especially with respect to its neglected artistic aspects. Real success will depend upon acting with the utmost effort and perseverance, since the task is one of bringing about a revival of art in building cities. This means discarding all of the trivial practices that dominate it today; the replacement of existing standards by their direct opposites.

Vision itself, the nature of perception of space, upon which every architectural effect depends, should be the basis for resolving all of the conflicting factors in city building. The eye is always at the converging point of a pyramid of visual lines extending from the object perceived, and various perceived objects are in a visual circle having the eye as its center, so that, with respect to the eye, they form a concave line. This is the natural basis of the principle of perspective that was so effectively used by the Baroque masters. Only by taking full account of the nature of perspective to make a maximum number of related objects perceptible at a single glance can we attain the best effects.

The modern block produces effects that work directly counter to the laws of perspective. The conflict may be most succinctly expressed by saying that art demands concavity while maximum land value insists upon convexity. The impasse could not become more absolute than it is now, but a good city plan can be produced without going to either extreme. Rather, taking into consideration the particular circumstances of each separate case, it should seek to reconcile the two extremes in measures that provide for economical development that can satisfy the requirements of artful arrangement. One of the best methods for accomplishing this has already been suggested; that is, emphasis on artful arrangement in the design of principal plazas and streets, with secondary areas planned for the most economical use of land. It may be shown, however, that rectangular plotting may, to a certain extent, be reconciled with art in city building. Figure 89 shows the placement of a church in the Baroque manner somewhat like that shown in Figure 90. The church (a) is built into other structures, and a fairly wide street opens into it. Its plaza is enclosed on three sides and has two suitable sites (g and h) for monuments or fountains. The adjoining buildings are: (b) the rectory which opens directly into the

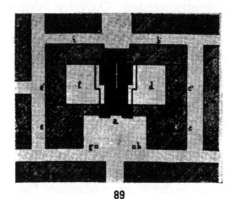

89

sacristy, and (c) a boy's school which provides access to church services without going out of doors in bad weather. The large court (d), separated from the church by a high wall, can be used for gymnastics. The other side could be used in the same way for a girl's school (e) with a kindergarten (f). The three remaining parcels (i, j, and k) could be used for dwellings or for additional school purposes. Both of the courts (d and f) could be made most attractive by trees, shrubs, and vines along the garden wall. Planting could also brighten the plaza or moderately long avenue opening behind the church.

This design has been purposely selected because it is readily adaptable to various kinds of administrative centers. The beauty of the calm, enclosed church plaza, the economy achieved by building the church against other buildings, and the accessibility of the church from school and rectory are obvious. Such an arrangement could be worked out for any small church with the usual structural appurtenances. A fine effect could be achieved by so grouping church, rectory, and school with perhaps a fountain, shrine, or small monument, with suitable planting and street arrangement.

The great urban communities grew up around market places dominated by city halls. Additional buildings like banks, brokerage houses, museums, markets, and stores were built around the square to form a structural ensemble. That developed a large structural mass subsequently divided into numerous tracts. A sufficiently large, almost square parcel would now be required for this kind of grouping under the

90

VIENNA:

Piaristenkirche
und Platz

prevailing block system. To strike off such an unfavorable site from the beginning would leave nothing for the architect to do except lay out interior courts within buildings that would inevitably assume the form of cubes, since each would have four similar façades of approximately the same height. The various buildings would not be visible from a single point of view, but would, rather, come into the line of a spectator's vision one after the other as he walked around corners. Thus the entire grouping of buildings would have cubic form, and there would be no opportunity to seek a maximum of effect with a minimum of cost. But if the architect who designs a major building also has a hand in planning the plaza and its surroundings from the beginning, the results can be quite different. He will be able to project a number of buildings, large and small, on the basis of existing needs, and he can group them around a concave line according to the laws of perspective. In that way he could give us plazas of outstanding interest instead of dark, void inner courts. Different conditions will suggest varied combinations, and the more freedom allowed the architect, the more power will he have to achieve picturesque groupings.

Those who prefer not to depart considerably from rectangular plotting may well consider the simple arrangement sketched in Figure 91. In this grouping the principal building (A), with a convenient entrance ramp, forms the end of a plaza (I) enclosed on three sides, with monuments, standards, or lamps on each side. B and C are secondary buildings joined to the principal building by colonnades (a and b). This simple yet superb plaza of stylistic regularity makes the best possible use of the three monumental façades that enclose it, all of which can be seen at a single glance. Posterior façades dominate the small plazas II and III, while plazas IV, V, and VI provide partial views of the principal façade. Under

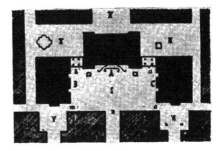

91

the block system all of these impressive elevations would be relegated to interior courts where nobody would see them. Each plaza in this group could bear its stamp of individuality. The main plaza (I) could be entirely enclosed by arcades incorporating the colonnades (a and b) with a fine resultant effect, for they could extend around the plaza without intersection, and the whole effect would be appreciable from a single point of view. Moreover, they would provide convenient access between plazas II and VI, and between III and V. A fountain could be placed in one of the two remaining plazas (II and III), with a monument in the other, to give distinct character to each. The smaller plazas (V and VI), withdrawn as they are from the principal line of traffic, have a special quality that lends itself excellently to restaurants or cafés with front terraces, or to towering monuments.

An arrangement of this kind is readily adaptable to a plan for the building complex of a great university, academy, or technical high school. For example, the chemical laboratory and other collections could be located on one side and the anatomical institute and medical faculty on the other, with the principal building in the middle. Certainly the architect's freedom to group buildings gives him a more fruitful opportunity than the thankless necessity of forcing everything into a clumsy cube form without projecting variations of any kind.

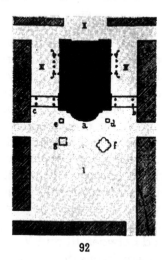

92

Now let us consider another example, the location of a theater. These buildings are usually left free-standing as a measure of protection against fire. However, by resorting to the use of arcades a theater can be used to form part of an enclosed plaza. Galleries could extend over the arcades on one or two levels to serve as emergency exits. If they are of fire-proof construction they

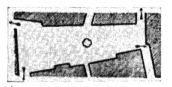

93

VIENNA:

New Market

would not endanger adjoining buildings. Finished in flagstone, they would, in fact, provide the most desirable kind of vantage points for the operation of fire fighting equipment. This blending of ancient principles with modern needs underlies the arrangement of a typical situation shown in Figure 92. The rounded projection (a) of the auditorium requires the withdrawal of building arcades (b and c), lamp standards (d and e), monument (g), and fountain (f) toward one end of the main plaza (I). The posterior façade of the theater could provide a valuable monumental wall to terminate Plaza II, while the important wide streets III and IV, from which entrance ramps give access to the theater, would provide the needed space for stationing vehicles without cluttering the main plaza.

All of these simple types, as we have said, have been purposely adapted as closely as possible to modern regularized plotting in order to demonstrate that enclosed plazas and other worthwhile features are attainable without excessive preparatory effort or impracticable expense. The essential needs lie in preserving enough free space to accommodate future buildings and for somewhat more favorable street extensions than are provided by the

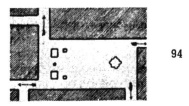

94

rectangular system. It will not be difficult to prepare in advance for every circumstance if care is taken to see that streets opening into plazas do not cut through them, as is the case in Figures 90, 91, and 92, but, on the contrary, take different directions in emanating from the plaza as shown in Figure 93. Application of this venerable principle would arrange street openings and locations for monuments or fountains in the usual small plaza in the manner indicated by Figure 94. It is applied even in the kind of rectangular plot shown in Figure 95. Such a variation in the block system would offer the additional advantages to the movement of vehicular traffic that accrue from street junctions as compared with intersections *(see pages 60-61)*. No greater mistake could be made, however, than to adopt this detail as a rigid practice in planning an entire city area. Avoidance of repetition of uniform pattern is a fundamental necessity, since stereotyped street designs

result in an intolerably commonplace and tiresome effect. It is important to get as much variety as possible into street design. A disposition of streets like that shown in Figure 95 should be employed only sparingly in places where there is likely to be a future complex of buildings with imposing plazas. Even the free arrangement of a suburban pattern would become boring if extended over too wide an area.

It is absolutely necessary to divide the movement of traffic only in those places where several streets converge at one point as in Figure 96. That invariably results in a poor plaza with respect both to vistas and traffic movement. This fair favorite of modern city building should be eliminated wherever it appears as a by-product of lot plotting, and the method for doing away with the weird phenomenon is quite simple. We simply need to put an irregular building site in the place of the irregular plaza as in Figure 97. This is but to follow the wise ancient practice of concealing unpleasant irregularities within built-over areas, and

95

thus within the walls of buildings, which effectively eliminates them.

The detailed solution of such a problem will naturally be different in each case.

When one or two principal streets converge on one of these points, they should be left undisturbed while the openings of secondary streets should be eliminated. These troublesome converging points can be avoided by changing the direction, curving, or breaking street lines. This would be of additional value in bringing about worth-

96

while irregularities in the street pattern which are so greatly needed to overcome the banal and all pervasive symmetry of the drawing board. Under some circumstances such a converging point could be replanned as a public park surrounded by houses.

The course of this investigation clearly indicates that there is no need to design modern city plans in the mechanical manner that has become common; that there is no need to exclude the splendor of art in building cities; and that there is no need to renounce the accomplishment of

the past. It is not true that modern traffic requires it. It is not true that public health requires it. Indifference and a lack of intelligence and good will condemn the modern city dweller to live his life out in a formless mass of monotonous dwellings and streets. It is true, of course, that the beneficent power of habit gradually dulls our senses to the impressions they receive, but how sadly this modern superficiality envelops us when we return from Florence or Venice! Perhaps that explains why the fortunate inhabitants of these cities that have been built

97

with such artful magnificence are rarely disposed to leave them, while we, on the other hand, must annually escape to take refuge in nature for a few weeks in order to endure the city for the rest of the year.

XII

IN THE last chapter we purposely considered only the simplest city building forms so that we might evaluate them according to the great standards of the past and suggest improvements. In this chapter we shall round off the study and bring it to a conclusion with an example in monumental style.

Perhaps Vienna, more than any other modern metropolis, makes an ideal subject for such a study. It has experienced an exceptional expansion that brought extraordinary expedients into use at a highly propitious time. Art and esthetics were flourishing throughout central Europe, while the attainments of the older Munich building period had reached their peak. The great ferment among the various schools of style had not subsided, and the proponents were in the happy state of high agitation. But the great work of the period was not born of zeal alone. There was prudent caution in action, and if actual accomplishment does not now appear to have fulfilled the lofty expectations of the era that planned it, we may be reconciled by the fact that nothing has been completely spoiled. That is contrary to common opinion, but careful investigation will bear it out. We should simply refuse to look upon an ungainly work as a complete work, however difficult it may be to remove its defects.

The imposing monumental buildings are, of course, structurally complete and offer no opportunity for alteration. We are fortunate to have them as they are, and consequently we would not wish to alter the buildings themselves, but look at the plazas and streets that surround them! They are all poorly and improperly laid out from the point of view of artful effect. Even so, the general plotting scheme, as part of the complete development, might have been much worse, even hopelessly irreclaimable, had not a certain degree of foresight been applied in it. The basis for a good present-day arrangement is rooted in three fundamental ideas that influenced the original development:

First, there was a general disposition to leave as much land as possible free of construction. This can assist us in working out improvements today.

Secondly, there was a tendency to follow the example of Paris in planning street extensions. This, too, made for more openness of arrangement. In many ways it recalled the Baroque style, as may be noted

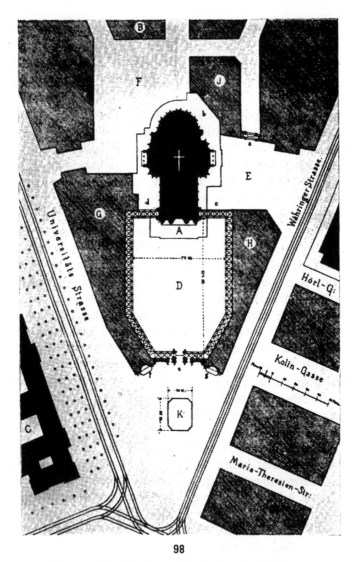

98

Proposed Replanning of the Votive Church Plaza

particularly in the perspective effect of the Schwarzenberg Palace and its plaza. Vienna with its models of original Baroque was more faithful to the style than was Paris where it was handled in a spurious, second-hand manner. But in fairness it should be said that this style was in disrepute at that time. It was the most despised of all styles, the very word "Baroque" having become a synonym for "corrupt," "ugly," or "degenerate."

Finally, the greatest organizational genius of the time was displayed by the deliberate manner in which the less important elements of development were begun first, to be followed by monumental structures, with the most striking building complex, the Court Museum and Palace, saved until the end. This employed foresight that proved to be sound in the light of subsequent developments, and in its clever handling of such an expanse of buildings it demonstrated consummate, matured artistic ability. Genuine ability guided by high purpose reached its zenith in the majestic plaza of the New Palace. The right planner appeared at the propitious moment.

That planner could have been found, and would have been found earlier, in the artist who was able to prepare such a grand plan for Dresden, except for the fact that Gottfried Semper was then in obscurity in Zurich, and his unrealized plan for Dresden was all but forgotten. Then too, it may be questioned, in view of the development of our art, whether a plan for city development done in the Semper manner would have been understood then, nor is it likely that its execution would have been supported, for there was widespread doubt as to the possibility of such coherence in building operations. The vision of that day was far more restricted than ours. A colossal plan of this kind, worked out in the ancient manner, would have been regarded as a Utopian dream. Execution had to await the ripening of time. When that came about the propitious moment was at hand, and Semper was called in. Had he been summoned earlier, his plan would have been too much for contemporary power of comprehension, and it would probably have remained on paper, whereas it is now progressing to a fortunate completion.

For all that, the present situation may be summarized as follows: buildings are well done; plotting is poor, but fortunately there is enough open space available to permit correction of the plotting errors. This can be shown most clearly in actual cases by means of sketches for the reorganization of part of Vienna's city plan without need for further description.

Figure 98 shows a design for the replanning of the plaza of the Votive Church. Under present conditions this is one of those wedge-shaped plazas, given over, with its broken enclosure, to all of the attendant mistakes. There is no distinction between the plaza and the streets (Währingerstrasse and Universitätstrasse). The plaza simply melts into its surroundings. There is no intimation of the kind of enclosed character that is so necessary to an artistic impression. Church, university, chemical laboratory, and the different blocks of houses stand detached, unsupported, and without collective effect. Placement of the various structures fails to draw from them a harmonious effect. Instead, each building seems to strike a different melody in a different key. The gothic Votive Church, the University in noblest Renaissance style, and the charmingly varied houses, seen in one view, produce the kind of effect that could be expected if a Bach fugue, the grand finale of a Mozart opera, and a couplet of Offenbach should be heard at one time. Intolerable! Positively intolerable! Consider what that would do to the nerves, to say nothing of its mere disagreeable quality! The juxtaposition of the house cupolas on Währingstrasse and the noble, delicate structure of the Votive Church produces a harsh effect that is just as intolerable. The façades of these houses are ably designed and stately enough in themselves, but they should not have been built opposite the Votive Church.

The obtrusive arched pagoda spires seem to outbid the nearby older cupolas for attention, giving a particularly unpleasant effect. How can we achieve a unified, artistic, well executed plaza effect, or any kind of worthwhile architectural effect, if each architect in his self-sufficiency seeks only to outdo the work of his colleague? This nullifies the collective effect of the plaza just as the effect of a dramatic scene would be ruined if the second and third bit players insisted on playing the principal role and could not be restrained by the director or monitor. We need the strong hand of a kind of monitor for building technique, and we need it most urgently because a mistake in the realm of architecture can not be easily corrected.

The situation described above, nevertheless, can be corrected by treating its second principal defect—its excessive size. The vastness of this empty space tends to reduce the effect of the magnificent church building to a minimum. Imagine the Votive Church on the site of Notre Dame of Paris or on the site of St. Stephan's at Vienna. What an impression would it then make! To reverse conditions, imagine St. Stephan's instead of the Votive Church on this formless, desolate monster plaza, and its effect would shrink to an extraordinary degree. We frequently hear the statement that the Votive Church is too small; that it looks like a miniature model; that it has an odd appearance from the side. Placement of the building and the awkward planning of the entirety are solely responsible for this. The explanation of the unsatisfactory appearance lies, not in the skilfully built building, but in the plaza. It has already been pointed out that a Gothic church should not be left free standing or located in a manner that permits an open and distant view of its profile.

This exposes the source of the trouble, and serves as the basis for proposing a remedy. Existing architectural effects must be kept separate from each other, and the beauty of the Votive Church must be given a proper setting according to the best practice in locating such buildings and according to the lessons of past success in planning church plazas. Appreciation of the exterior of a Gothic church requires an appropriate plaza form based on a square of depth before the principal façade with its lofty towers. There should be a separate, distinct plaza for the side elevation to separate the view of the high towers from the view of the asymmetrical, oblique slope of the choir. Finally, the chapel crowns are best set off to be seen at an angle, for that gives a fine perspective of the buttresses and numerous pinnacles.

The great expanse of open space in this case makes it possible to fulfill these conditions today as may be seen in Figure 98. This shows a large atrium to provide a proper setting for the principal façade of the church, and, by means of buildings erected on parcels G and H, to isolate the building from its unfavorable surroundings. The plaza would then be 246 feet wide (wider by one-half than St. Mark's) and 341 feet long, dimensions which are still too great in comparison with fine old examples of church plazas. The atrium would be, like ancient models, a quadratic plaza, and the length of its flanks would not be much greater than the width of the church façade. The overwhelming majority of old church plazas cover as much area as is covered by the church building itself, but a plaza approximately three times as expansive may be planned if the utmost in size and stateliness is desired. A plaza larger than that would be out of proportion to the structure and would diminish its effect. The atrium in this case (D) would assume these maximum dimensions, which is justified by the maximum dimensions of the adjacent streets, and maximum dimensions in everything which may be seen here in accordance to the prevailing custom. The Gothic arcade to surround the atrium should be carefully worked out in every detail to conform to the style of the church (naturally in stone) with precaution to see that it remains subordinate to the church façade. For this reason the arcade should be as high and slender as is consistent with a single story, while the structural groupings G and H behind the arcade should be just high enough to obstruct a view of the disturbing tin cupolas beyond them. This new building should be worked out so that the building height is relatively low on the side toward the atrium, and high on the side toward the street. The entrances c, d, and e, with the corners of the plaza, could be designed to give the entire enclosure a monumental effect. The long sides of the plaza could be gradually embellished with monuments, frescoes, and the like, so that finally the place would be abundant in works of art like the renowned Campo Santo at Pisa and others of the kind. The remaining area of such a fine plaza would also be appropriate for numerous large and small monuments, whereas the existing formless expanse has no suitable sites for them. One or two fountains might well be located here, for they have belonged to the atrium since ancient times. They should be placed in the area immediately in front of the church but in a manner that leaves a wide, unobstructed corridor in the central axis from e to A. Large trees and shrubbery might appropriately be planted along the sloping sides from e, the principal entrance.

Even the recreational value of this atrium would be greater than the present widely spread and purposeless arrangement, due to proper development rather than to dimensions. Hygienic considerations, which are generally brought to the defense of excessive openness, can scarcely justify the present arrangement of the plaza. It is intolerably exposed to high wind, inclement weather, heat, and dust, as well as to the din of the streets, and the incessant clanging of trams. Consequently it is usually deserted. On the other hand, the proposed atrium, protected against wind and dust, segregated from the bustle of the streets, with shady, quiet retreat in the arcades and planted area near the principal entrance, would surely attract a willing public seeking relaxation. For that reason it would be well to permit shops, especially for light refreshments, in the sloping walkways near the entrance, e. With proper supervision other needed places might be located near the other entrances. For the sake of maintaining clean air direct connections between the plaza and street movement should be avoided. A small waiting room might be built in one of the structural groupings (G and H) and made accessible from the arcade. This kind of development would make the atrium much more valuable from a hygienic standpoint than the present expansive and poorly arranged plaza. The reader who has the inclination may judge the artistic value of the present plaza for himself.

Artists can find solutions to conditions like these and thereby provide an occasion for the investment of artistic capital in a city plan. The conditions must be stated in a manner that can draw forth artistic solutions, for if we begin with conditions that specify a block layout we can not be surprised if artistic solutions fail to develop.

Buildings on G would extend Universitätstrasse before the buildings standing opposite, and the structural mass on H would bring Währingerstrasse down past the houses. This demarks the part of the entire plan that adjoins the Ringstrasse. The entrance, e, should be worked out as a monumental arched portal, not in Gothic style, but, on the exterior, in the best Italian Renaissance like the University, for both portal and University will be seen simultaneously. Style unity conforming to the inside of the atrium is unnecessary since this outer architecture and the Gothic Votive Church with the Gothic arcade could never be seen at the same time. Conflict in style would thus be resolved by moving the boundary line between styles to the interior of a wall—the same expedient that can be used to conceal irregularities in building sites. We should always follow the principle of harmonizing everything that may be seen in one view, and we need not concern ourselves with that which cannot be seen. That is the road to practical effect, and it will never lead us astray.

Emplacements for large fountains would be appropriate at f and g near the large archway at e. The present plaza is so immense that even when all this has been carried out there will still be an open area in front of the atrium large enough to serve as a site for the Votive Church itself. Thus it would be appropriate to locate a monument of the greatest dimensions in it at K. Assuming that such a monument could have the projected architectural background (from f to g) its effect would attract the sketch books of countless artists.

Problems of meeting other requirements in the plan are simpler. They seem to solve themselves. Building on the parcel J, with the archway a, begins the formation of a desirable plaza (E) to set off the lateral façade. The archway (a) is on the proper side of the church to provide the best lateral view, and it harmonizes with the entrance (c) to the atrium without producing a tiresome, stiff, symmetrical effect, which would be inappropriate to the form of the plaza as well as to the asymmetrical church eleva-

tion. The area at (b) should be as narrow as possible and, for the sake of contrast with the more expansive plazas, there should be no passage through it. The same should apply to the area at (d). Adjacent construction should be brought up as closely as possible to the church, so that its two identical lateral façades could present two different impressions—a free-standing effect in one instance and a snug, built-in effect in the other. This would correspond to the placement of most old cathedrals. It would provide distinctly different approaches to the atrium at (c) and (d). There would be four portals through the arcade at one entrance and only three on the other.

It may be thought that the prelacy should be moved from B to F and connected directly with the church. There can be no objection to this from a purely artistic point of view. Plaza F serves to enhance the view of the chapel crown, the final stipulation of the problem, but it is, perhaps, not essential.

The City Hall Plaza (Figure 99) presents a similar problem. Open space extends in every direction from the so-called plaza which is without enclosed character or cohesion. There is simply no plaza effect or artistic effect of any kind. Again, there is too much open space. We can readily imagine the impression of immensity that the new City Hall would make if it were fitted more closely into surrounding building, but in its present situation it does not appear to be as large as it actually is. This is an invariable source of disappointment to

101

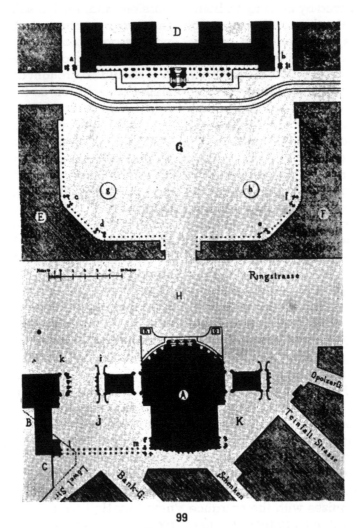

99

Proposed Replanning of the City Hall Plaza

strangers who usually say that the building is not as imposing as its pictures had led them to believe.

There is a single viewpoint at one side from which the building seems to grow to gigantic proportions. If the plan had, in advance, been exactly reversed with respect to the Ringstrasse its effect would be like a view through a magnifying glass, so much so that the apparent grandeur due to the effect of contrast would be more convincing than the judgment of the eyes. Undoubtedly the City Hall of Vienna should have an enclosed plaza of expanse with limited dimensions and appropriate stylistic treatment.

The present situation of the new Burgtheater *(Figure 99)* is even more unfortunate. What abundant effects could have been derived by the old masters from such a glorious structure with its monumental façades! The different parts of the structure —on one side a great hall, on the other a theater—halfway form a marvelous plaza. But where is the other half?

The plaza (K) on the side toward Teinfaltstrasse is irremediable. The back façade, which might have served admirably as the enclosing wall of a plaza, is similarly lost to advantageous use. Only the side toward Lowelstrasse can now be used in the formation of an attractive plaza, for here alone is there enough open space. Such a plan could do away with the present isolation of the structural entirety which stands at present without cohesion, like an erratic block. Its

poorest effect, however, is presented by the principal façade toward Ringstrasse. In this case the ground plan of the building requires completely different surroundings. The rounded protrusion needs compensatory treatment in the entrance area between (n) and (o) and some recession from street traffic. At present, instead of this, a street railway track runs closely by with annoying obtrusiveness. The resultant sensation is as oppressive as the habit some men have of constantly closing in upon persons with whom they are conversing until, at length, they seize the very coat buttons of their listeners. If we withdraw, the offender follows until his very nose is almost upon us. Unquestionably, we breathe more freely when we are relieved of the oppressiveness.

The tramway produces that kind of oppressiveness here where a certain free openness is essential. Thus, the tramway could best be removed and relocated to run in Reichsratstrasse from the Votive Church to the Parliament House and by the City Hall, and this could be done without detrimental effect to development along its line.

These are the problems to be met in designing plazas in this area, and they have led to the plan shown in Figure 99.

Partial building up of the large open spaces could produce a City Hall Square (G) of character. This is wholly a problem in utilizing the architecture of the City Hall —the given element—to permit development of true originality. This could be accomplished by extending the form of the

103

lateral arcades of the City Hall around the entire plaza. In connection with this, four corner towers erected at c, d, e, and f would complement the City Hall façade. The corner towers built into the arcade should be of small dimensions and less imposing in design in order to accent the powerful effect of the City Hall. For the same reason, buildings on the parcels E and F should not be built to the full height of the typical Vienna rent house. They should be, rather, one or two stories lower. At H the plaza wall, which also serves as an enclosing wall to Ringstrasse, should be opened to permit a vista upon the tower from A. Triumphal arches at (a) and (b) could be crowned with monuments similar to those of Scaliger at Verona but of larger size. The middle arch might bear an equestrian statue, perhaps of some hero of Vienna's defense against the Turks. Other smaller monuments could be located in front of the corner towers at c, d, e, and f, and in fact along the entire circumference of the plaza. Fountains could be located on the sites (g) and (h), but it would be even better to put permanent concert pavilions there for regular musical programs. A large café could be provided for on one side, with a restaurant on the other side. Obviously this type of development would eliminate the present style conflict which arises from the varying architectural treatment of different buildings that may be seen simultaneously.

The formation of Plaza J is also explained by the plan. The symmetry of the theater building suggests the structural addition (B) (for administrative offices or for some independent purpose), which extends slightly into the park (C). This could be connected with the theater by a colonnade from (l) to (m), the upper level of which could give access to and from the theater. The areas at (n) and (o) provide prominent and appropriate sites for large monuments.

The manner in which the proposed arrangement extends to the University in one direction and to the Parliament House in the other is shown in Figure 101.

Two similar parcels on either side of the City Hall are used in this plan to enhance the approach to the principal façades of the University and the Parliament House which front on Ringstrasse. This was a happy solution although it required some compromise with convenience, since the approach could not be made as expansive as might have been desired. The present situation of the Parliament House is especially awkward, requiring a struggle to reach the building from the Ringstrasse. There can be no doubt that the inadequacies of this place in the development of the City from the Court Museum to the Votive Church are attributable to the Ringstrasse. This is certainly true in the case of the University. It should have a quiet, dignified plaza worked out in a manner appropriate to the building, but this is scarcely possible now. On the other hand the Parliament House is sufficiently withdrawn from the street to allow for remedy. It would scarcely be possible to find a more striking example of inexpediency and conflict between building and plaza than this. The architectural features and detail of the building put it in the style classification of the so-called Greek Renaissance. However, the general grouping of the structural parts (middle section, connected corner sections, approach, and small garden enclosures) unmistakably indicate a full-fledged and exceptional Baroque layout, of which the ancient Greeks had not the slightest foreboding.

Thus in the Parliament House we

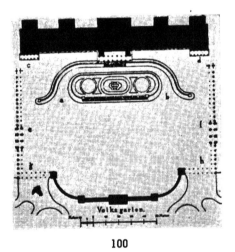

100

Plan for a Plaza before the Parliament House, Vienna

have the essentials of a Baroque building with its characteristic formal garden *(See Figure 100, from a to b)*. But where is the general form so essential to these features? Can we withhold from a building designed for powerful perspective effect a foreground

that permits an adequate view? It is unthinkable, but that is precisely what is done by modern city building in its absolute inability to understand the necessities of art, to say nothing of its inability to satisfy them. Only gradual conditioning to this situation makes it tolerable to us. In terms of art, the harsh conflict is intolerable. The Ringstrasse must be kept at a distance from this building, which must be given a foreground plaza. When this is done the building will, for the first time, unfold its full charm. We can get a faint idea of the possible result by looking at this splendid structure in winter between leafless trees from the Temple of Theseus across the expanse of the Ringstrasse. It may be said that the City of Vienna has never seen its Parliament House at its best, for the proper viewpoints are spoiled by the Ringstrasse. It is exactly as though one should hang a fine tapestry with its face to the wall. The architectural beauty of the structure is simply not put in its proper setting along this segment of the Ringstrasse, and the result is that its power and expression remain unrealized. It is still possible to improve conditions in this case. In Figure 100 one attempt at improvement is sketched.

The open areas would be enclosed by colonnades on both sides, from (c) to (g) and from (d) to (h). They would be of one-level construction and they would be brought to the height of the ground floor level of the Parliament House. They should be given a Romanesque treatment on the

105

outside corresponding to the style of the building. Within, they should be of columnar design with horizontal entablature. Essentially this would be following the treatment of old city gates, except that it calls for less massive construction with closer adherence to the form and dimensions of the Parliament House.

There should be an attic on both sides to correspond in relief and embellishment to the principal building. It should be segmented by triumphal arches at (e) and (f) which would bear elevated quadrigae like those of the principal building. Open access to the park would be provided at the entrances (g) and (h). This would also provide a welcome thoroughfare from the plaza to the inner city, which will be needed in the future. Such a plaza would permit a more expansive approach to the building than was originally planned, and it would provide locations for splendid monuments.

A small slice from the park opposite the Parliament House could produce this superior plaza, which, in turn, would provide sites for great monuments, and permit superior treatment of the original architectural grouping. Although this would be an advantageous type of development, it is the kind of work that is seldom undertaken today.

As we continue along the way from the Votive Church to the Court Museum, as it is at present, there remains a final unrhythmic place—the wedge-shaped plaza of the Palace of Justice. This, too, owes its origin to the bending of the Ringstrasse polygons and the accompanying breaching of rectangular plotting in this particular area. This ugly triangular form is found in nearly every new city, and for the same reason. In no instance has it resulted in development of beauty. There is no formula for improving such plazas. They should be built over.

In this case it seems best to build so that structures face the Ringstrasse and back toward the Palace of Justice in a four cornered plaza *(XI in Figure 101)*, with the foremost "point" of the building in imposing rounded form.

The diameter of the rounded part of the building could be made great enough to obtain a truly striking effect. As sketched in Figure 101, it is 164 feet, and thus greater than that of the Mausoleum of Augustus in Rome, if less than that of the immense Mausoleum of Hadrian (now Castle of St. Angelo), which is 240 feet.

This building should be worked out in the best architectural style to harmonize with the nearby Court Museum. The problem, then, is to bring this kind of arrangement into the present situation. Another question arises as to the purpose to be served by such a building. It is difficult to think of this place as a site for rent houses. Its form at once suggests a use as a mausoleum or as a crypt with adjoining cloisters, but it could also serve as a museum or auditorium.

It is well known that no suitable place

101

COMPOSITE PLAN

Explanation

Plazas

I, II, IV. New Plazas Adjacent to the Votive Church
III. Atrium of the Votive Church
V. University Plaza
VI. City Hall Plaza
VII. Large Plaza of the Theater
VIII. Small Plaza of the Theater
IX. Plaza of the Parliament House
X. Garden Plaza
XI. Plaza of the Palace of Justice
XII. New Palace Square

Buildings

g. Proposed Addition to Burgtheater
h. Temple of Theseus
j. Site for Statue of Goethe
k. Unspecified New Construction
l. Palace of Justice
m. New Wing of Imperial Palace
n. Proposed Triumphal Arch
a. Chemical Laboratory
b. Votive Church
c. Site for Large Monument
d. University
e. City Hall
f. Burgtheater

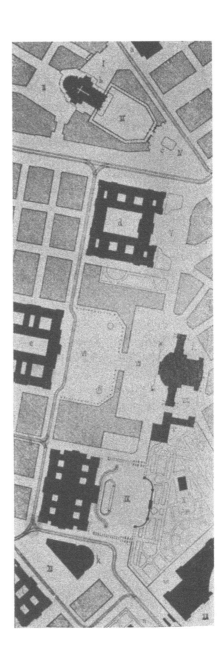

for a Mercantile Museum has been found in the center of the City, and there have been complaints of the lack of a Concert Hall. We will not find plazas for them in the clouds. We must rather put them in places which practical considerations indicate as suitable for them, and in that way we can arrive at worth while city arrangement.

Results of the complete study are shown in the composite plan *(Figure 101)*. While it shows the proposed new route of the tramway, it does not show the suggested connection with the Wahringer branch behind the Votive Church in Schwarzpanier Street, which is outside of the area sketched. This would permit the making of connections in all directions with just as much convenience as is the case at present, and it would shift the movement of traffic in a way that would change it from a nuisance to a utility.

Benefits of this rearrangement would be: (1) elimination of conflict in architectural style; (2) enhancement of the effect of each monumental building; (3) a group of plazas with character and individuality; and (4) a suitable location for assembling numerous large, medium, and small monuments.

Each new plaza would provide a new vista. Nearest to the majestic new Palace Square (XII), truly grandiose imperial forum, would be the fore plaza of the Parliament, a kind of regal forum (IX) worked out in classical spirit. Appurtenant to the building that houses the Parliament, this plaza could become an artistic symbol of the imperial spirit, and this should govern the choice of monuments that would be gradually assembled in it.

A kind of cupola of foliage might be worked out close by the park opposite the Temple of Theseus (h), which could serve as an appropriate location for the proposed monument to Goethe. This plaza, too, would have a quality about it to suggest the forum and the ancient manner. With the beautiful park and the mausoleum-like building (k), this plaza would have the effect of grouping a number of harmonious works in a sufficiently close proximity to meet stylistic requirements while, at the same time, keeping each building separate.

A few steps from this plaza could take the observer into entirely different surroundings of the plazas of the theater (VII and VIII), where it would be appropriate to put up monuments in honor of great writers and artists. Still another completely different and distinct picture would be presented by the City Hall Plaza (VI) with its Gothic arcade. Monuments erected here could appropriately be given over to the memory of persons who have been famous in the history of the City.

It is even possible to provide a fore plaza for the University Buildings that could strikingly enhance the effect of the fine portico, if the monotonous line of the Ringstrasse is moved back, with the space thus gained filled in with massive groupings of trees and shrubs.

A completely distinct and individual impression would be presented by the Atrium of the Votive Church. Monuments to men of learning would be most appropriate in this quiet, peaceful place.

Thus, this series of plazas would bring into being suitable sites for monuments according to the character of each, while at present there is not one suitable location for a monument in the area due to the excessive openness of arrangement.

This explanation may be considered as an illustration of the manner in which artistic results can be achieved in the monumental center of a great city by following the teachings of history and the examples of beautiful old cities. Other solutions may be possible, but the same fundamentals and methods must be adhered to unless art is to be renounced from the beginning.

XIII

THUS far there have been some experiments in bringing the old manner of city building with forum-like plazas into modern favor. Artists and architects are enthusiastically restoring ancient plazas, and this work, to which we are indebted for many splendid glimpses at a vanished ideal, indicates that accomplishment of equal beauty is within the reach of our time.

All of the recent experiments have one element in common. They are all on paper only. Thirty years ago, E. Forster, in his biography of the architect J. G. Muller (page 39), wrote:

> "The fact that most of the new large buildings in Munich were isolated and, consequently, without the combined effect that could have been attained by grouping, despite their deficiencies and inconsistencies, led Muller to advocate the planning of a single plaza on which cathedral, city hall, library, exchange, and other like buildings might be grouped."

We can readily understand why this purely academic plan was never carried out, since it was proposed only as an illustrative study. Later, however, in 1848, Muller participated in a competition for the *bas fonds* of the Rue Royale in Brussels by submitting a plan in the manner of the ancient forum. The plan was excellently developed, highly esteemed, but never carried out.

We have already mentioned the fate of G. Semper's plan for Dresden which met the destiny that seems to hover over all attempts at art in city building in our time, but it did excite a lively interest in influential circles, and there was even a start toward carrying it out. But the plan, although begun under such apparently favorable auspices, will not be successful. A certain courageous spirit underlies works of that kind which run counter to past experience. One might almost persuade himself that our excessively prosaic generation is simply incapable of greatness or beauty in this particular province.

Perhaps, however, as has been suggested, a lucky star hovers over the Vienna plan. We cannot expect colossal new development in Vienna. The monumental part of the city is completed, leaving only lighter and less important structures to serve as the material for producing the proper framework. The main element—the picture—is ready. Only the frame for it is lacking. There is something compelling in this state of things that should mean that sooner or later the solution will, and must, come forth. Regardless of when this may happen, it seems possible to foresee that it will produce a magnificent, forum-like plaza—a new Plaza of the Palace—which, in fact, is already nearing completion. In the majesty of its conception it will surpass anything that has been done since the building of St. Peter's at Rome.

Should this not, then, give us new courage? To some extent it is possible to forecast its development. This one accomplishment is well under way, and the time is not far distant when the second, opposite development will be undertaken. The old palace gate will go with the completion of the new palace building, and that will, in time, bring into being a great and magnificent plaza. That will mark the decisive moment for determining the future of the whole arrangement—the time for dealing with the two planned, arch-like closings of the Ringstrasse, which can, for the first time, bring artistic unity into the whole grouping. Undoubtedly it will then be necessary to project an enclosure of consistent style toward the imperial stables by extending the entire lower half of the Court Museum in corresponding architectural style.

The feeling of immensity, which even now is engendered by this plaza, will certainly exert a strong esthetic restraint. Surely the formless wedge-shaped plaza before the Palace of Justice and the whole of the remaining plaza confusion around the Parliament buildings will not be much

longer endured. When something does happen here it should be directed toward the production of a great and model plaza for the new Palace.

The problem then will not be one of dealing with the pros and cons of opinion, as we may expect a general agreement on this. It will be, rather, the problem of finding the means by which other buildings may be brought to completion. This should entail no great difficulty, for by that time Vienna will have a much greater population than it has now; there will have been very little new building in the center, as is evident from the sketch outlined; and productive private purposes will require a number of large parcels for new building. The yield of these building sites will be sufficient to defray the cost of the requisite arcades so that there will remain only the basic question as to whether or not such an arrangement will be harmonious.

To the layman this may seem to be a difficult decision to make, for if the experiment in building up these parcels should fail, the result would be a great misfortune, with the existing buildings left to stand as they are. This permits a concrete suggestion, not for castles in the air, but for the definite procedure suggested here, which is quite practicable, not only in this instance but for application elsewhere. We might select, for example, one feature such as the atrium before the Votive Church for a demonstration of general practice in building church plazas and make a temporary exhibition model of it from boards and plaster. It could be accurately built to show the effect of the planned building up of the open area. This would enable everyone, including laymen, to appraise the value of the new effect, and to express a worthwhile opinion as to whether or not the proposed development should be undertaken. The technician can readily guarantee the propriety of the project from the plan.

Under no circumstances should the building parcels be given over to the unrestricted use of the purchasers, either in this instance or in the areas proposed for development around the City Hall Plaza. That would certainly spoil everything from the start, since each of the different architects would attempt to put his competitors in the shade. Rather, all plans for joint building should be prepared in advance so that there may be an attempt at achieving the desired harmonious collective effect, with everything subordinated to the effect of the principal building. An obligation should attach to every parcel requiring development without essential departure from the established plan. This is the lesson of recent development which indicates that we cannot expect this kind of benefit through any other means. This is especially necessary today when there are so many predilections in style and tendencies in taste, with nobody particularly concerned about his neighbor; much more necessary than in ancient times, when there was as yet no debate as to style, and buildings seemed to fall into good

collective arrangement without constraint.

The bare text of a few standards given to the prospective owner as a kind of dowry can scarcely be expected to suffice in such a difficult situation. The weirdest kind of invasions could probably break through even the most stringent general standards. The procedure we have suggested could determine the manner of carrying out the building operation. An actual example, such as we have given, can clarify the problem much more readily than can academic theories on the nature of artistic city building.

Other types of regulation should be dealt with in the same manner. For example, the archways in Vienna which determine the formation of the Schwarzenberg Plaza, the Plaza of St. Charles' Church, and the Freihaus or the eventual parcelling out of the Linienwall area, should be regarded not merely as technical problems, but also as artistic matters of supreme importance.

Certainly the fact that we are approaching these problems with more responsibility and deliberation than was the case a few decades ago is evidence that we are accumulating more experience in this province. With all of the recognized mistakes, as well as the good examples, that are at hand, a heavy guilt must be assumed today by anyone who spoils a city plan. There is no necessity for glossing over the problem now as there was a few decades ago when cities suddenly began to grow

Conclusion

in undreamed of ways, and when adequate powers for coping with this onset were lacking. Every technician engaged in site planning today has an obligation to give careful consideration to every factor, including the artistic factor, and it is to be hoped that the still customary block pattern as a plan for city development will be finally cast aside by its remaining sluggard adherents. With greater respect given to the artistic phase of city building, especially in the conduct of competitions, we can develop greater artistic powers, and we shall be able to accomplish many fine things even though the high ideal of the ancients may remain unattainable to us for the calculable future.

NEARLY twenty years ago the Princeton Architectural Association offered to make it possible for Nils Hammerstrand to translate Sitte's masterpiece; but at that time the University had to decline the offer because the task had already been pre-empted by another scholar who apparently never completed it. Perhaps in the late twenties little attention would have been paid to Sitte's *artistic foundations* by an America obsessed with the speculative mania and well satisfied that its mushroom urban growth was both natural and healthy.

Today, however, there is no question about Sitte's timeliness. We have learned our lessons and are ready to admit that there has been something radically wrong in the type of controls which have shaped the growth of our metropolitan areas, and even our smaller cities. The brief penetrating note by Charles Stewart, who made the present translation, contains real food for thought. As he makes clear, had there been some understanding of Sitte in America before the adoption in 1916 of the first Zoning Ordinance by New York, perhaps Ameri-

cans might have avoided some of the mistakes of the great building boom.

Our greatest fault has been that we were unconscious of the type and source of controls which were moulding our destiny. We were naive enough to believe that mushroom growth was the natural course of city development.

Those who really controlled city growth were the surveyors who laid out rectangular streets and lots and the lawyers who composed the descriptions and obligations that were written into deeds and mortgage contracts.

Americans accepted these limitations meekly and were slow to realize that the legal documents which "protected their rights" on the one hand deprived them on the other of the liberty of planning for proper group relationships. Not so with Sitte; he assails the "geometricians" who depended upon T-square and triangle. He decries the interminable vistas; the buildings, all parallel, facing on streets of unvaried width. He speaks of the lack of understanding of the need for out-of-door enclosed space so arranged as to give the citizens a consciousness of and an appreciation of the function of the buildings which face upon out-of-door enclosures.

Sitte's artistic fundamentals contribute a meaning to the design and growth of cities. One must confess, nevertheless, that to a large number of Americans the use of the term "artistic" may convey an idea of superficiality. Unfortunately we have been led to think that, since artistic merit is so frequently judged by the eye, it is a merit that is the result of surface appearances rather than the result of inherent fundamentals. It is partly for this reason that American cities have been shaped more by engineering decisions than by decisions based upon artistic fundamentals. Unfortunately, when engineering is only half understood it is even more superficial than art can be when understanding of fundamentals is lacking.

The rectilinear street system was usually imposed by ill-equipped engineers who were afraid to transcribe or lay out more complicated relationships. When engineers of this type superimposed a gridiron pattern on an uneven terrain, they got around the difficulties by recommending that the grades be changed to fit the plan, ignoring the fact that cut and fill, though relatively inexpensive on a drawing board, may often be extravagant in reality. Of course there are great advantages in straight streets and in level streets, but not when carried to interminable lengths, nor when unrelieved by changes in width or other interruptions.

Once introduced, there was a secondary reason for the popularity of the rectilinear street system. It was easily susceptible of division into marketable standard building lots. During the period of most rapid growth, the extension of American cities was largely financed by the sale of building lots. The varied functions to which the design of the city should have been adapted were subordinated to the idea of land and homes considered as exchangeable merchandise.

A glance at some of the efforts to correct past errors reveals the need for understanding artistic fundamentals. For example, zoning regulations were introduced to protect property on the one hand and the public interest on the other. But to assure the constitutionality of zoning, ordinances were so worded as to make the provisions uniformly applicable to the properties affected. Zoning laws established uniform "protective" set-back lines for private residences. Instead of producing harmony in design, the result has been to accentuate the damage already done by the exaggerated parallelism of the street. The houses have been made to elbow one another like long lines of soldiers standing at right-dress. Practically no improvement in the distribution of space was thereby effected. On the contrary, to assure the maintenance of one's legal rights, it was necessary to build up to legal limits, especially at the front of the lot. This prevented concert in planning and tended to choke expression of the relationship between neighboring properties.

115

Sitte had absolutely no experience with skyscraper architecture. It is improbable that he ever expected that our cities would be encumbered by great masses of tall buildings. This was one reason for his criticism of "large" squares. He contended that they tended to dwarf the mass of the buildings. Nevertheless, the principles which Sitte laid down are as fully applicable today to the enlarged masses of modern cities as they were to the market squares of Roman times or the plazas of medieval commercial Italy.

Were it not for the spaces left between the high buildings by properties on which low buildings still stand, the skyscrapers of lower Manhattan would be well nigh unbearable. For a moment let us think of this space between the upper stories of the skyscrapers as a fortuitous and perhaps unconscious application of Sitte's artistic fundamentals. The pedestrian at street

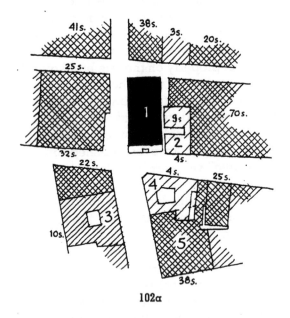

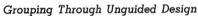

102a

Grouping Through Unguided Design

1. U. S. Subtreasury
2. U. S. Assay Office — 4 and 9 stories
3. N. Y. Stock Exchange — 10 stories
4. J. P. Morgan & Co. — 4 stories
5. Equitable Trust Co. — 38 stories

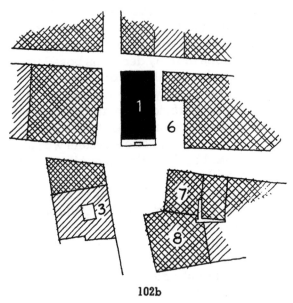

102b

Grouping Approximating Sitte's Principles

1. U. S. Subtreasury
3. N. Y. Stock Exchange
6. Open space
7. Suggested alternate site for J. P. Morgan & Co.
8. Smaller site for Equitable Trust Co.

level, however, is still lost between long lines of parallel façades. Now let us imagine that it were possible discreetly to eliminate some of the less useful and often obsolete lower structures. No longer would we have buildings ranged in meaningless parallel rows. We would achieve open spaces between buildings. The pedestrian would find relief from long tunnel-like streets. Small open plazas would give meaning to the relationship of the buildings facing upon them. These outdoor spaces would provide improved outlook, as well as light and air for the occupants, who live and work behind building walls.

For example, had the principles of Sitte been fully appreciated in America at the time the elder J. P. Morgan was projecting his new banking house in New York, it is unlikely that he would have permitted his architects to plan a structure crowding out to the extremity of the lot which he owned. Had the Morgan Bank been set back and the Assay office (whose usefulness was to be short lived) been omitted altogether, we should have had an application of artistic fundamentals, as can be seen in the drawing, that would have added material as well as esthetic value to the neighborhood.

Although Sitte devotes a great deal of space to the design of the plaza, he continually refers to the need of satisfying the impression produced upon the eye. He was never an enthusiast for the French School, which sought to develop great vistas and long distance axes. In Sitte's day the work of Baron Haussmann was the outstanding European example of planning in the grand manner. In America Major Pierre Charles L'Enfant, who had been trained in the earlier French School of the 18th Century, was given the commission of creating a new capital city. He made a plan which depended upon grand vistas. L'Enfant, and especially the successors of L'Enfant, in their enthusiasm for vistas and angles, gave insufficient thought to the importance of the grouping of buildings to express human scale and human relationships. The great avenues, circles, and squares of Washington are bordered by notoriously bad building sites. The planning of the space between buildings has been, to say the least, incoherent.

I should like to cite a particular instance taken from the planning of Washington, as carried out by the successors of L'Enfant, where one of the principles enunciated by Sitte would, if followed, have given infinitely greater artistic merit to one of the greatest monuments of modern times, namely the Lincoln Memorial designed by Henry Bacon.

The Washington Monument had already been located off the intersection of the two principal axes of the Mall. In the revised plan of Washington the offset was "corrected" to give the illusion that the monument was on axis. When the Lincoln Memorial was located, instead of adopting the bent axis advocated by Sitte for long vistas, the Memorial was placed on a prolongation of the line of the Washington Monument and Capitol. As a result, the visitor emerging from the Lincoln Memorial finds the dome of the Capitol blotted out by the shaft of the Washington Monument. Had the axis been bent and the Washington Monument kept off the center, the visitor could have been made visually conscious in one moment of the relationship between the Nation's Capitol and the monuments of two of its greatest heroes. Unfortunately, because of failure to understand artistic fundamentals, the visitor will never be able to emerge from the Lincoln Memorial chamber and look past the shaft of the Washington Monument to the dome of the capitol beyond.

The more is the pity because the French school of planning for long vistas on the grand scale is dependent upon momentary impressions derived at the instant of approach and departure. Sitte wrote at a time when grand distances and incoherent spaces had deprived men of a sense of contact with architecture. He strove to make architecture the interpreter of human relations which it ought to be.

It was Sitte's contention that fundamentals, though long neglected, can be uncovered. Even the gridiron pattern of the modern American city is not hopeless. Space can be opened up. Design can be achieved by thinking more of the grouping of buildings and by planning for the out-

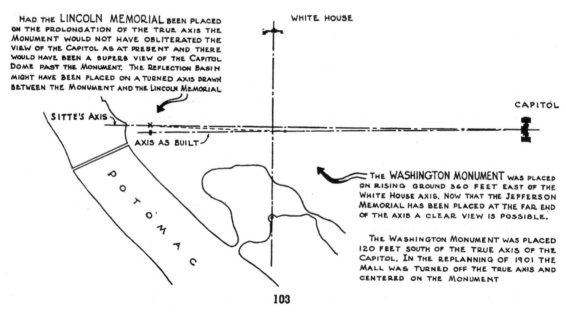

HAD THE LINCOLN MEMORIAL BEEN PLACED ON THE PROLONGATION OF THE TRUE AXIS THE MONUMENT WOULD NOT HAVE OBLITERATED THE VIEW OF THE CAPITOL AS AT PRESENT AND THERE WOULD HAVE BEEN A SUPERB VIEW OF THE CAPITOL DOME PAST THE MONUMENT. THE REFLECTION BASIN MIGHT HAVE BEEN PLACED ON A TURNED AXIS DRAWN BETWEEN THE MONUMENT AND THE LINCOLN MEMORIAL

WHITE HOUSE

CAPITOL

SITTE'S AXIS

AXIS AS BUILT

P O T O M A C

THE WASHINGTON MONUMENT WAS PLACED ON RISING GROUND 360 FEET EAST OF THE WHITE HOUSE AXIS. NOW THAT THE JEFFERSON MEMORIAL HAS BEEN PLACED AT THE FAR END OF THE AXIS A CLEAR VIEW IS POSSIBLE.

THE WASHINGTON MONUMENT WAS PLACED 120 FEET SOUTH OF THE TRUE AXIS OF THE CAPITOL. IN THE REPLANNING OF 1901 THE MALL WAS TURNED OFF THE TRUE AXIS AND CENTERED ON THE MONUMENT

103

door space between them than by confining our efforts to the design of individual façades which can never be seen anyway except as part of unrelated compositions. See illustration of replanning of Bloomsbury by London County Council.

Let us throw away the horse-blinders which architects have worn to shut out the rest of the city while they wasted a disproportionate amount of their energy on street frontage alone. Perhaps it is this waste of energy on a type of design which does not seem to matter in the hodge-podge of the modern city that has given so large a percentage of the public a regrettably limited understanding of the fuller services which the architects could render, if they based their work, as Sitte urged, upon the artistic fundamentals of city building.

When once the thread of artistic tradition* has been severed, whether we realize it or not, man through habit will follow such other traditions as he is able to recognize. Let us ask ourselves what sort of tradition we have been following. If we can understand the forces which direct our actions, we may find that the outlook for the modern city is not hopeless. Having lost contact with Sitte's artistic fundamentals, perhaps we have been groping blindly, following the path of engineering trivialities. At this point we must stress the difference between the fundamentals of engineering and engineering trivialities. In its fundamentals, engineering is as much an art as architec-

*See page 82.

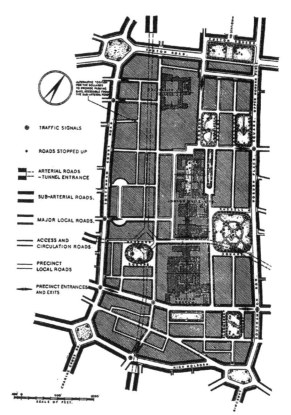

London County Council Plan for University Precinct, Bloomsbury.

Courtesy Macmillan and Co., Ltd., London

ture. Men who are guided by engineering fundamentals are on sound artistic ground.

Let us picture for a moment a street of detached homes for the medium income group in any of our modern cities. Between the side walls there is a space of perhaps eight to fifteen feet. Why are houses so placed that the side windows look directly

119

at the walls of the adjoining buildings? Most houses of this type are built for sale. Would they not be more salable and better to live in if they were planned as a group to give each householder more light, air, and outlook? Strange as it may seem, the average developer has preferred uniformity of placement on the lot, as giving him the advantages of uniformity and economy in water, gas, electricity, and sewer connection, and enabling the man with the instrument who lays out the houses on the lots to complete his work in less time than if he had to work to an irregular plan. Thus, in his zeal for understanding without understanding of fundamentals, the developer has practiced a false economy.

Although Sitte has pointed out the objectionable results of streets laid out by geometricians, and certainly residential streets have suffered in this regard, he does not specifically discuss the design of residential neighborhoods. Nevertheless, the artistic fundamentals discussed by Sitte in connection with public squares may be found to be applicable to the design of space between residences, even between the type known as "small homes." It is here that the lawyers and salesmen have offered resistance more difficult to overcome even than that of the geometricians. If homes are to be grouped around an open space and that space is to be given, by the skillful arrangement of the masses of the buildings and the growth of trees and shrubs, the feeling of an out-of-doors room, then assuredly the harmony of the out-of-doors space cannot be maintained unless neighbors concede certain rights of mutual enjoyment to one another. It is this type of communal planning for common enjoyment that is often frowned upon by lawyers and salesmen, because it complicates sales. They even object to common runs of sewers and branch water lines because they make properties interdependent, hence less free for exploitation. By preventing the exploitation of land (which means the overdevelopment or abuse of particular pieces of land) the incentive to buy and sell land for speculative profit is greatly reduced. Sitte's charge that the geometricians have played into the hands of the salesmen is well founded. The developers of cities have lost the tradition which bound them to artistic and engineering fundamentals and have followed instead the tradition of artistic and engineering trivialities. Enough damage has been done, one would think, in the half century since Sitte wrote, to cause Americans of today to heed the warning and return to fundamentals.

Author's Preface

The pros and cons of various city planning systems have become pressing questions of the time. In this, as in all current issues, opinions of wide variance are being expressed. In general, however, there is a widespread favorable recognition of the great technical accomplishment that has come about in transportation, in the development of building sites, and especially in hygienic improvement. In contrast to this, there is an equally widespread rejection, even ridicule and contempt, of the artistic failure of modern city building. Although much has been accomplished in the realm of the technical, what we have achieved in the artistic is next to nothing. Our noblest monumental buildings generally stand in badly conceived settings and awkward surroundings.

This has been our motive for studying the arrangement of fine old plazas, or public squares, and the plans of magnificent ancient cities to discover the elements of their beauty, so that those elements might be set forth in a summary of principles which, properly understood, could be employed to produce equally fine effects. This being the guiding purpose, the work is neither a history of city building nor a polemical piece. The object, rather, is to contribute a résumé of practices and principles to the great body of practical esthetics that can be followed by the practicing city planner.

There is included a quantity of valuable illustrative material, particularly of city plan detail, which has been set up, as far as possible, to a uniform scale. In some cases, where this was not possible, average dimensions of at least approximate accuracy have been used. The examples have been taken from Austria, Germany, Italy, and France, since the author follows the principle of speaking only of cities that he has seen and observed for their artistic worth. This principle alone makes it possible to produce a worthwhile, useful work, and distinguishes it from the exhaustive comprehensiveness of a history of city building.

C. SITTE

Vienna, May 7, 1889

Preface to the Second Edition

The first printing of the book was completely exhausted within a few weeks after its appearance. This is gratifying evidence that our purpose of stimulating an active interest is being accomplished. The time for precise judgment is not yet at hand, and there appears to be no need at present for expanding the material presented in the original edition. This second edition, therefore, appears without change.

THE AUTHOR

Vienna, June 1889

Preface to the Third Edition

The fundamental idea of this book—sending city building to school to nature and to the ancients—has, since its publication, been impressively translated into practice in a manner that is supremely gratifying and, to the pessimistic author, most surprising. Some eminent colleagues have been outspoken in their statements that through this work an entire new trend in building cities will be started. This should be put in its proper light. A literary effort can produce such an effect only when, so to speak, the air is charged with its subject. We may not expect such gratifying results until there is a general feeling and understanding that in some way finds clear expression. As this does not depend upon the elaboration of detail, the third edition is appearing in unchanged form.

THE AUTHOR

Vienna, August 24, 1900

Preface to the Fourth Edition

In 1902 *The Art of Building Cities* appeared in French as *L'Art de Bâtir les Villes*, translated and completed by Camille Martin. Our father took this occasion to make some revision for a new edition in German, which is followed in this fourth edition. The article "City Vegetation" which thus far has been available only to a small circle of readers, is added as an appendix.** Plans of the Acropolis of Athens and the Forum Romanum, with some examples of the latest scientific research have also been added. Some of the ground plans have been worked over and as far as possible perspective drawings have been replaced with photographs,** but within the meaning of the prefaces to the two preceding editions, the work as it appears in this issue remains unaltered.

SIEGFRIED *and* HEINRICH SITTE*

Vienna, December, 1908

*Camillo Sitte died November 16, 1903
**Not included in this English translation.

INDEX

125

THIS book was set on the Linotype. Memphis Medium type was used for the text matter. Though based on a century old Egyptian design, Linotype Memphis is far removed from its crude ancestors. A true contemporary face and the reflection of our scientific times, it combines the simplicity of functional form with the style smartness useful for books of an architectural nature. The classic type used throughout jacket, cover, title page, and heads is known as Copperplate Gothic, a type used by the printers of medieval times.

The illustrations from the original German edition have been reproduced in this book. Printed by Ar-Kay Printing Company, Inc., New York.

Lightning Source UK Ltd.
Milton Keynes UK
UKHW030622200919

350146UK00004B/573/P

9 781614 275244